An Eagle Nation

Volume 24
SUN TRACKS
An American Indian Literary Series

Series Editor
Ofelia Zepeda

Editorial Committee
Vine Deloria, Jr.
Larry Evers
Joy Harjo
N. Scott Momaday
Emory Sekaquaptewa
Leslie Marmon Silko

An Eagle Nation
Carter Revard

The University of Arizona Press

Tucson

The University of Arizona Press
Copyright © 1993
Carter C. Revard
All Rights Reserved   r

☉ This book is printed on acid-free, archival-quality paper.
Manufactured in the United States of America

98 97 96 95 94 93   6 5 4 3 2 1

Library of Congress Cataloging-in-Publication Data
Revard, Carter.
An eagle nation / Carter Revard.
p.   cm. — (Sun tracks ; v. 24)
ISBN 0-8165-1355-4 (acid-free). — ISBN 0-8165-1403-8 (pbk. : acid-free)
1. Osage Indians—Poetry. 1. Title. II. Series.
PS501.S85   vol. 24
[PS3568.E784]
810.8 s—dc20   93-12720
[811'.54]   CIP

British Library Cataloguing-in-Publication Data
A catalogue record for this book is available from the British Library.

This Book
is
for the Wazhazhe and Ponca Nations
and all our Relations:

Tha-ghi^n ge no^n pa-hi,
No^n-pe-wa-the ge no^n shka-hi.

Wah-leh-zeh o-ksheh-toh^n bree^n tha-ha
Ee-ko-a-bah o-weh-nah-beh
zha-zheh No^n-peh-wah-theh
ah^n-kue-beh.

Contents

Sea-Changes

Acknowledgments

Some of the work in this collection has been published in the following places: *Caliban* ("A Cardinal, New Snow, and Some Firewood," and "In Oklahoma"); *Voices of the Rainbow* (Viking Press, 1975: "Not Just Yet," "But Still in Israel's Paths They Shine," "North of Santa Monica," and "January 15 as a National Holiday"); *Denver Quarterly* ("The Country's," here retitled "As Brer Coyote Said"); *Contact II* and *Nuke Chronicles* ("Statement on Energy Policy"); *The Chariton Review* ("Foetal Research"); *West Coast Review* ("Outside in St. Louis," "Outside in Oxford"); *Earth Power Coming* (Navajo Community College Press: three poems inserted into the prose piece "Report to the Nation: Reclaiming Europe"—"Rock Shelters," "Over by Fairfax, Leaving Tracks," and "Stone Age"); *Poetry East* ("What the Eagle Fan Says" and "Communing Before Supermarkets"); *River Styx Magazine* ("Close Encounters," "In the Changing Light"); *Indian Youth of America Newsletter* ("Eagles, Drums, and a Ponca Elder," here titled "An Eagle Nation"); *Studies in American Indian Literature* ("Birch Canoe," "An Eagle Nation"); *Calapooya Collage* ("The Readie and Easie Way," "A Response to Terrorists," "The Man Lee Harvey Oswald Missed," "Moccasins for Christophoros"); *Nimrod* ("October, Isle of Skye," "Letter to Friends on the Isle of Skye," "November In Washington D.C."); and *The Webster Review* ("Earth and Diamonds"). I thank them for permission to reprint.

A Giveaway Special

We are given this world and some time with friends. How time dawned on mind and was beaded into language amazes me the way an orb-spider's web or computer-chip does, or the dance of time and space and energy that patterned selves into my parents, who did not have me in mind, and into the four children and seven grandchildren who've so far surprised us. Amazing that a brief quivering of air can re-present such wonders, that little coded curves of ink on paper might set the same vibrations pulsing from a human mouth in Buck Creek, Oklahoma, and from others in Singapore or some future meadow or unbuilt spaceship—from mouths now neatly packed into genes that have not even begun to express themselves as human parts, within their unripe sperm and ova. The creation of language, of writing, is less astounding than the invention of water, but not much less, and we each re-create, as we go, all that has been given us, changing silently the meaning of a word so we can talk about the American robin in front of us as well as the English robin behind us, so that friends will listen for how a word-creature sings in America, now, not how it sang in England, then. Under the old names, new beings gather; within the new beings, old ways survive.

So here we float in time among the stars, given these depths to surf on, swim or drown in, or just to see (as one Laker said) "that uncertain heaven received / Into the bosom of the steady lake"— or language, or mind. As *Proverbs* puts it: "As in the water face answereth to face, so the heart of one person to another." I quote from memory, whose ripples may not have caught those Blue Angel words in their true Dove shapes.

All this portentous stuff is to say I am grateful that water and language, time and space, memory and writing, have been given us— and I've set their star-stuff into the best poems I could for you who hold this book. At the powwow, when I said to Don White at his trader's booth that I had only been able to honor one of the people with a blanket, he looked at me in a way that put my remark in its place and said: "Remember, you're just one small person." The world does not NEED honor from poets, and all we can give is not enough anyhow. I know this, but here are some of the things I can give, and some of the people I want to give them to. They are not named in any particular order, but as they come to mind, and I apologize for having so little to show my appreciation. Maybe at a future occasion I can do better.

I thank Kaye Norton for spicy help; sons Lawrence and Geoffrey for unserpenting the Apple, our daughter Vanessa for an interesting life, our son Stephen for many surprises of the better sort; Naomi for illuminating the page, Stanley for making the darkness laugh; my sister Josephine for rising above it all on muleback, my brother Jim for prime time in Oklahoma; my cousin Roy, brother Antwine, and buddy Walter for saving me from drowning here and there in Buck Creek; Stella for starlight, grandchildren for mornings; cats for cathedrals (why not? perfection/purrfection); THE professors, Eikenberry and Hayden, for how and why and wherewithal; Oxford for time past; Uncle Woody for many times and many lives—not ONE for the FBI! My Irish folks for calling me Mike O'Toole, my Osage folks for naming me Nompehwahthe. My Uncle Arthur for ignoring the tornado and painting a bedroom orchid purple, my Uncle Bert for knocking down the man who insulted our mother, my Uncle Dwain for paving U.S. 60 and pipelining Oklahoma, fighting in North Africa and brawling in Pawhuska and Ponca City.

I should thank inlaws for much good sense, outlaws for many good stories; Uncle Carter for that lightning ride, on our pinto half-Arabian mare Beauty, over the new green bluestem; Grandpa Aleck for Beauty, for grandfathering, for profane Honesty. My mother for us and this world. Uncle Aubrey for grapes, a teddybear, bootlegging and slick card dealing. Mr. and Mrs. Dillahanty for the hayfields, the barn lofts, pickups, tractor rides and trust, home cooking and sweet well-water. Mort and Rosalie Murray, Gordon and Julia Wells, Otto and Eunice Yount, Guy Bockius and Mae, Grif Graham and Orpha. Toby and Joe riding the stallion Stardust, Dave Ware and his foxhounds, and the Osage County Wolfhunters telling lies over campfires and firewater. Porky Starks and his dad, the handsomest Creeks and handiest with fists in the Territory. Glenda Stark, whom Faulkner named Eula, and her blond blue-eyed brothers, her tough no-nonsense mother, down by Sand Creek's pebbly sandy ford above the springhole. Harry and Rose Carpenter making work for me and offering to help me through college though I turned them down, determined not to be "helped." Mister Kendall and cherry-lipped Mrs. Kendall and their platinum blonde kids, from Johnny Greyhound Marine down to the twins; and High Border and Drumhurlin Border and Upside Down and Osage Border and all the greased lightning greyhounds we trained. The Popes, the Templetons, and the James family whose handsome father so courteously, one velvet summer night, came to the door of their house in the Green Valley's deep bluestem, and let in three lovesick boys for long enough to glimpse his beautiful daughter who brought us cake and glasses of milk and showed a Patrician graciousness before we left to walk the three miles back to our home and wonder if she suspected. The Dillon kids, assuring us they were immune to poison ivy as they rubbed on their faces the vine-leaves curtaining a dry waterfall near their house, way off in Sand Creek woods—and not coming to school for a week while they calomined and moaned. My cousin Roy for teaching me to read, make beanie-flippers, to spell "eave," and not to taste any more ripe olives straight off the tree, no matter how plausibly he praises their glorious taste that you just never get out of a bottle of olives.

And I ought to give thanks for that taste for trivia questions and the elocution lessons that Mrs. Fisher drove me to, hell for leather over every bump in the back streets of Bartlesville, when I was in first grade, a taste that got me a Higher Education via the University of Tulsa's radio quiz scholarship. And it was my twin sister's lobbying that got me nominated to try for that lottery. And what of my sister Josie's great beautiful tragic eyes, and her tomboy mastery of the Lone Ranger music in our games, even before she was allowed to ride the blood bay quarterhorse mare that Mr. Chism, old cowboy turned barber who bought the forty acres northwest of us, had trained to stand still while he, after his stroke, climbed painfully aboard to ride her across our meadow a half-mile to the mailbox every day. My stepfather Addison, who strode into a half-mile square of hip-deep corn with a hoe and day by day chopped down its weeds and softened its loam, all this after walking the mile and a half to work at sunrise, and before going home in the dusk among fireflies. My brother Antwine, the night we sneaked the car out of our garage, pushed it down to the highway and started it, damning its missing muffler, wobbling all the way in to Bartlesville with three dollars to spend, and just missed slamming into somebody who ran a stop sign, then in the all-night greasy spoon heard the drunk man in top hat with a cane calling people cocksuckers until we slipped out and drove back, easing the loud car into the garage with its lights off and going in where we knew our mother, deaf as she was, had probably marked our going out and our coming in. And the other time he and Walter Parks and I drove in on a Memorial night and saw the two drunks in an old Chevy coupe smash into the back of a parked truck with no rear lights, the car jamming under the truck's steel bed so the driver could get out of his door but the passenger had his ribs crushed and throat cut, and we watched him banging his head and gasping, saw the blood coursing down from the slashed throat suddenly stop and knew he had died, pinned between seat and windshield. We had been passed a block away by the coupe, blatting way over speed limit with its cutouts open, and the driver hanging an arm out and banging the door as they went. When the cops showed up, finally, the driver said it was the dead man who had been driving, and nobody said any different. We were not supposed to be there, so we left. . . .

—And Les and Edna and Frank Baker and Mr. Tayrien for blackberries, strawberries, coon hunts, epic all-nighters down Sand Creek, and back again to folks who thought we'd drowned and spanked some of us for it. Grandma Josephine for camping and fishing on Grand Lake, for giving me a name, for introducing me to spring-fed flint-rocky streams so cold I couldn't duck under, being used to warm brown water—and for Christmases, and a longer summer. Uncle Kenneth, for the softball games, for his poems and sports columns, for floorboarding it all the way. Aunt Arita, for restoring my memory. Flora and Ivan and Michael and Meredith, on Pacific beaches, at Pawhuska dances; Mr. Logan, for prayers and history. For the Lookouts and Braves and Warriors, Pittses, Redcorns, St. Johns, for John Joseph Mathews and his stories of night flying and misdirected bombs, for Raymond and Peggy, Julia and Vonnie. For the Red Eagles, and for the Klash Kah She meetings that the women went to. For the peyote times of which Add said, when I asked him had he taken peyote, well yes he had but no more, because he was talking to these people and they weren't even there. . . .

For Quentin, warming the drum at Hominy and telling an outrageous joke from his time in England before D-Day; and for Hazel whose folks gave the Osage ceremonies that are in the Bureau of American Ethnology monographs: Hazel speaking, remembering, in quiet tears praying in Osage, and then at the In-lon-shka when she invited us to eat with her and Quentin, the hilarious stories she and Aunt Jewell told of escapades in their teens, when they got so sick first chewing tobacco.

And for my beloved Aunt Jewell and the thousands of Poncas in her family, our family, starting with the six great cousins, of whom more in *Ponca War Dancers* and in *Cowboys and Indians, Christmas Shopping*, for whom Frank Parman, Renegade himself, has made books to hold them like the Arena bench and chairs at the Ponca Powwow. For my Ponca uncles Gus and Johnny, my aunts Hattie and Ruby, some of whom once, hitchhiking, caught a ride with Pretty Boy Floyd on his way to or from a bank for withdrawal. For Sarah and Frank, and Richard and Cammie and Joe Dale. For Ben and Peggy, good neighbors without fences, and the best story of how the Amherst bunch hired a Harvard guy that will ever be told, unless Ben tells another. For Wendy and Arthur, Linda and Joy and Rainy Dawn and Krista Rae and Simon, for Paula and Larry and Norma and Jerry. For Janie Bell and Anita, Rosalie and Mary Ellen and Mrs. Parks the best Christian I know, and the two French girls from Damar, Kansas, who let Walter and me walk five miles home down the railroad track as the dawn brightened. And what was the name of Walt's kissing cousin that summer in Palco? Or the men we talked to through the third floor jail window of the courthouse in Russell (or was it Fort Hays?), Kansas, that we had climbed up to on the outside stonework? Or the bronc rider killed that afternoon at the rodeo where I was reading Housman's "To An Athlete Dying Young" from the copy of *A Shropshire Lad* that I had bought in the little bookstore that morning while we were trudging round trying to land a job on an oil rig after the wheat harvest had passed on north. Or the guy who married the town floozy and they stayed three days and nights up in their top floor bedroom while he tried to do enough, and then he went to work on the highway crew and she was at the town's main drugstore next Saturday night waiting for the redheaded guy with his Lincoln v-12 to come by, some ten days after we had given the groom a great shivaree that ended with throwing him in the water-trough after a chase through the WHOLE TOWN, all three streets AND cross streets of it. What was the word he had passed down from that third floor when the inlaws took up a hot meal on the third day and asked when they would be coming down—"We're living on love," I think he said.

And for Merton College, darts and beer and rowing, doing a "war-dance" around St. Alban's Quad one night after the punch had been spiked with neat brandy, trying to match the New Zealand philologist who was doing a Maori Haaka, and shouting "Bugger the tutorials AND the tutors!" up at the windows of Fellows Quad where the dons may not have been amused, a night that had only two serious results—first the bust-head morning when our stairway scout told us what it would cost to clean up, and then the sober day next term when the Warden of Rhodes House asked politely whether it was true, as he had heard from a friend at Merton, that I was part Osage. Message received, so next time we had a Bump Supper I took the wardance elsewhere, climbing over the Long Wall into Magdalen College where—as those with better memories say—they held the Vice President of Magdalen over a fishpond till he said that our boat did not deserve to be bumped by the lucky Magdalen eight. But that, I think, was BEFORE we went down to wreck the Balliol Boathouse and saw, across the Isis, the sanguinary Sons of Balliol seemingly intent on wrecking the Merton Boathouse. It was well past midnight by then, so my friend Ian McMichael, with whom I jumped into the river to swim over and rescue our Boathouse, should not have been so surprised when, halfway over and feeling very sleepy and warm in my heavy flannel clothes—this was, I think, an English March night—I told him that I was going to take a nap and would finish swimming across later. He insisted on towing me shoreward, so I went ahead and swam, but by the time we got across and walked back upstream, the Boathouse area was deserted, and nothing damaged. I am grateful to Mac for his good advice, which may have saved our boathouse and certainly saved me.

And the St. Louis Indian Community: George and Laverne Coon, Clifford and Marge Walker, Paul and Phyllis Calcaterra, Terry Packineau and Warren Comby, Charlotte Highley and Dana Klar, Louis and Gene and the Jordans. . . . Most of all the Voelkers, to Bob and

Evelyne, Kateri and Bill and Robert and Lee, who have taught me more of Indian ways than anyone but my Osage and Ponca folks, and given me new friends—Dale and Lez and Lynn and Jay and Mark and Allen. . . . The circles come round in such ways that in 1991, when my beloved Aunt Jewell was being interviewed for the NEH by Evelyne Wahkinney Voelker, they discovered that back in the 1930's it was Aunt Jewell's brother, Uncle Gus, greatest of Ponca dancers, who had helped outfit and teach to dance Evelyne's older brother Rusty, now a good singer and sometime Head Man Dancer. Uncle Gus, during the Anadarko dances, would stay with the Wahkinneys when Rusty was a boy and Evelyne a baby. Now in 1991, Evelyne was Director of the American Indian Center of Mid-America where I was President of its Board of Directors, and I had introduced her to Aunt Jewell when my cousin Casey was Head Lady Dancer for our Powwow. Evelyne's folks gave a beautiful Eagle Banner to my cousin Dwain (it has by now been carried up at the Sun Dance on the Rosebud)—and then we discovered that sixty years before, Uncle Gus and Evelyne's father were good friends, and Gus had helped her brother Rusty. Now again, Ponca and Osage and Comanche people became relatives in the Indian way, an Eagle Nation as my cousin Carter said in the small Pipe Ceremony when he and Craig and the family thanked the Voelkers for the great honor of the Eagle Banner, given them as veterans of Wounded Knee.

And my brother Addison Jump Junior, and Grace and Kim and Aaron there near King George, Virginia, telling the Tomahawk missiles (I think) where to go. When they came to visit, we went up in the St. Louis Gateway Arch and looked down at the Mississippi waters flowing past from Montana and Minnesota, and we came down and crossed the Mississippi to the Cahokia Monument and climbed up Monks Mound, where a pre-Columbian nation had maintained for longer than the U.S.A. has existed the largest town north of Mexico City, bigger than London at that time I believe. From Monks Mound we could see the Arch and St. Louis clearly, but from the Arch we could not see Monks Mound, which may say something about Indian vision, or about European eyesight. It was, however, on a day of partial solar eclipse, so maybe the view from the Arch is better in full sunlight, though I doubt it.

And this is also for Michael and Dee, and Jan, for Duff's and

the River Styx, for Eugene and Shirley and Quincy and the great
singers of East St. Louis; for Danny and Denver and David, Jaybird
and Connie and Anita, Rendy and Marie and all the Deans. For Joe
and Maud and Frankie, for the eagles of Skye and mosses and ravens,
amber pools and silver waterfalls, guitars and chess, daisies and
sheep, castles and ceilidhs.

A giveaway, I know, is for a family or those who have done some-
thing very special for the person who, in giving them what he or
she can, tries to express the honor he feels for these people. It might
be a blanket that is given, or a basket of groceries, a shawl, or all of
these and more. We have been given much more; we are small beings
given this great world of time and space, and as humans we have
been given all that our ancestors made for us in the language we use.
And then we live and move every day not just in bodies, in sight and
hearing and feeling, but in houses, buildings, whose builders shaped
and joined their parts, moved the stones and timber, hammered and
backhoed and ran the concrete, shingled and tarred, linked up the
pipes and wires. Those workers have seen to it that we who come
after them can be dry, are warmed or cooled as the seasons require,
can turn a tap and drink pure water, can push a switch and read in
light from fossil plants millions of years old or from the breaking of
atoms that had been gyroscoping since the universe began. I know
there are homeless people, I remember the cold of an Oklahoma
winter when we went hungry for three days of snow, it is not to cele-
brate the luxury of a Kuwaiti palace that I am giving these words. It
is just to say: each of us has been honored before we were born, we
are here in the circle where all the old people have placed us, here
where the stones and stars and grass and trees, all our relatives, have
danced before us and are dancing with us to the old songs. All the
beings touched by these words are dancing among the stars, not only
the waves and the light are dancing: "You have waited, you always
wait, you dumb beautiful ministers," as Whitman sang, crossing
Brooklyn Ferry. So I want to give away to those who have done all
this for me, and who will be listening and speaking with me perhaps
in a century from now, what I can give.

So here then is my giveaway, as special as I can make it, and I hope
it carries the honor I feel for those who read with a good heart and
a good feeling. I appreciate your coming a long way to this dance

with us, where we could have a good time and go around the drum together. You are welcome in my books at any time, and if you are going home now, or wherever you are going, I hope you have a safe journey and a good life, and you live into the happy days, *ho^n-ba tha-gthi^n*.

An Eagle Nation

In Oklahoma

When you leave a Real City, as Gertrude Stein did, and go to Oakland, as she did, you can say, as she did, there is no there, there. When you are a Hartford insurance executive, as Wallace Stevens was, and you have never been to Oklahoma, as he had not, you can invent people to dance there, as he did, and you can name them Bonnie and Josie. But a THERE depends on how, in the beginning, the wind breathes upon its surface. Shh: amethyst, sapphire. Lead. Crystal mirror. See, a cow-pond in Oklahoma. Under willows now, so the Osage man fishing there is in the shade. A bobwhite whistles from his fencepost, a hundred yards south of the pond. A muskrat-head draws a nest of Vs up to the pond's apex, loses them there in the reeds and sedges where a redwing blackbird, with gold and scarlet epaulets flashing, perches on the jiggly buttonwood branch. Purple martins skim the pond, dip and sip, veer and swoop, check, pounce, crisscross each other's flashing paths. His wife in the Indian Hospital with cancer. Children in various unhappiness. White clouds sail slowly across the pure blue pond. Turtles poke their heads up, watch the Indian man casting, reeling, casting, reeling. A bass strikes, is hooked, fights, is reeled in, pulls away again, is drawn back, dragged ashore, put on the stringer. In Oklahoma, Wally, here is Josie's father. Something that is going to be nothing, but isn't. Watch: now he takes the bass home, cleans and fries it. Shall I tell you a secret, Gert? You have to be there before it's there. Daddy, would you pass them a plate of fish? See friends, it's not a flyover here. Come down from your planes and you'll understand. Here.

Not Just Yet

This burly son of a bitch,
when we got outside the beerjoint
he moved between me and the light
and loomed up close and said,
"Think you can whip me, do you?"
I couldn't see well, facing the bright light.
"She don't want to dance with you," I said.
He reached his hand out, laid it on my shoulder,
and pulled the other fist back.
"My brother's got a tire-tool, over there," I said.
He took a step back, looked sideways
and saw Jim holding the tire-iron
there by our car and watching us.
"Grady," he said, loud over his shoulder,
"I want a little help, here."
A gray-haired drunk with glasses
climbed out of his Ford's front seat
and a sagging blonde came with him.
He was holding the snub-nosed pistol
loose in his right hand.
"You just go right ahead, Billy Don," he said,
"Betty and me can dance when you're finished.
There won't nobody interrupt you any."
That was when headlights came around the curve
and shone in my face.
"Here comes that god damn state patrolman, Grady.
Better put the gun up," Billy Don said.
Before the black-and-white car had pulled up and parked
they'd gone inside
and had the juke-box playing
the "Long Gone Lonesome Blues"
and Billy Don was dancing
half buried in the sagging blonde
when the state patrolman went in.

Over by Fairfax, Leaving Tracks

for Mike and Casey and the Kids

The storm's left
this fresh blue sky, over
Salt Creek running brown
and quick, and a huge tiger
swallowtail tasting the brilliant
orange flowers beside our trail.
Lightning and thunder've spread
a clean sheet of water over
these last-night possum tracks
straight-walking like a dinosaur in
the mud, and next to these we've
left stippled tracks from soles made
in Hong Kong, maybe with Osage oil.
Lawrence and Wesley pick blue-speckled flints
along our path, one Ponca boy
in braids, one part Osage
in cowboy hat.
Over the blue Pacific, green Atlantic we
have come together here; possum's
the oldest furred being in this New World,
we're newest in his Old World.
Far older, though,
and younger too, the tiger swallowtail has
gone sailing from those orange flowers to
sky-blue nectar: the wild morning
glories
will spring up where she's touched, marking
her next year's trail.
Makes me wonder,
if archaeologists should ever dig these prints
with possum's here, whether they'll see
the winged beings who moved
in brightness near us, leaving no tracks except
in flowers and
these winged words.

Rock Shelters

For John Joseph Mathews

Up here, bluff-slabs of sandstone
hang out from the rim,
painted bluegray with lichens, sheer
over dusty level of a
sheltered place: water sometimes
down over places worn and knobby drips
and darkens, softens earth to hold our
lifeprints; buttercup and rock pink
live where the hickory's branches fight
the sun and wind for power, but mostly here's
just humus: leaf-mulch deep and rustling
between great boulders broken from rimrock sliding
invisibly down the steep slope. The walk
down through these to the creek that
runs some of the year below here,
thin and clear over silty sandstone's
edges and angles, is short, steep, shady. Stoop
back beneath this shelter, we're in dust,
but in this damp earth just outside
the overhang are mussel shells—
                              worn
to flaky whiteness, rainbow of
iridescence long since dead. Here's charcoal too,
deep under the hanging slab. See,
            we were
                        once here.
Moving with Doe Creek down
to where it joins Buck Creek,
down this narrow shallow canyon choked
with rocks you come out where
the trees loom higher, elm and pinoak columns
rise and arch dark over earth
loamy and loose and the creekbanks
of steep sandy clay, roots jutting over pools

muckbottomed winding down to Buck Creek and
mingling where it moves from
sandy shallows down to springfed depths
and darkness.
Here, the winter
surrounded deer and turkeys, here lived plenty
of beaver, muskrat, mink and raccoon, fox and
bobcat and cottontail, coyote slinking, quail
and squirrels, mice and weasels all with
small birds watching from the bush and grapevine, berry
tangles, juncoes, waxwings, cardinals like blood on
snow, all sheltered here from
the prairie blizzards north.
And southward, in the bend of
Buck Creek level to the southern ridge a valley
of bluestem grass thigh-deep under
sunflowers nodding, meadowlarks flying and singing with
grazing buffalo, red wolves and coyotes trotting watching
with pricked ears a hunter crawl with
bow and arrows for a shot.
Now crossed
by asphalt road, wire fences, lanes to white farmhouses
where no farming's done, grapes and lettuce and
bananas on the polished table from Texas, from
California, Nicaragua, the orange-fleshed
watermelons that once lay in sandy fields by
Doe Creek gone as truckloads of melons rumble
past from Louisiana into town where food is
kept. To plant here, you buy. This land
was needed, we were told, it would be used. So oil is
pulsing from beneath it, floats dead
rainbows on Buck Creek and draws its brief trails
straight as a Roman road across the sky where people sit
drinking and eating quietly the flesh of what
has followed buffaloes to winter in
the valleys underneath, on which
sky-travellers look down.

This new world
was endless, centered everywhere, our study
of place and peoples dangerous, surprising, never
completed. Doe Creek
tasted different from Buck Creek and our people still
did not look all alike.
How far, meant counting
the streams that must be crossed.
The reasons why were everywhere, uncircumscribed;
stars twinkle, moon never does, they both
were relative to whippoorwill and owl.
Greenwich did not
keep time for us. The small stars now
move fast and send down messages of war
to speech machines or pictures of
pleasure to our living rooms, inviting us out into
a larger endlessness with many
centers. Galaxies, before long, may
be sold for profit, once the first space ship has
claimed one and the next has
come to kill all those before. Think
of walking on blue
stars like this one, new
plants, new beings, all the rock
shelters where we'll crouch and see
new valleys from.
Here is my
mussel-shell. Here is the charcoal.
We were here.

Apache, Omaha, Osage, Choctaw, Micmac, Cherokee, Oglala . . . .
Our place was ninety-fifth,
and when we got there with our ribbon shirts
and drum and singers on the trailer,
women in shawls and traditional dresses,
we looked into the muzzle of
an Army howitzer in front of us.
"Hey, Cliff," I said, "haven't seen guns that big
since we were in Wounded Knee."
Cliff carried the new American flag
donated by another post; Cliff prays
in Omaha for us, being chairman
of our Pow-Wow Committee, and his prayers
keep us together, helped
by hard work from the rest of course.
"They'll move that 105 ahead," Cliff said.
They did, but then the cavalry arrived.
No kidding, there was this troop outfitted
with Civil War style uniforms and carbines
on horseback, metal clopping on
the asphalt street, and there
on jackets were the insignia:
the 7th Cavalry, George Custer's bunch.
"Cliff," Walt said, "they think you're Sitting Bull."
"Just watch out where you're stepping, Walt,"
Cliff said. "Those pooper-scoopers
will not be working when the parade begins."
"Us women walking behind the trailer
will have to step around it all
so much, they'll think we're dancing,"
was all that Sherry said.
                            We followed
the yellow line, and here and there
some fake war-whoops came out to us

from sidewalk faces, but applause
moved with us when the singers started,
and we got our banner seen announcing
this year's Pow-Wow in June,
free to the public in Jefferson Barracks Park,
where the dragoons were quartered for the Indian Wars.
When we had passed the judging stand
and pulled off to the little park all
green and daffodilly under the misting rain,
we put the shawls and clothing in the car
and went back to the Indian Center, while
Cliff and George Coon went out and got
some chicken from the Colonel
that tasted great, given the temporary
absence of buffalo here in the
Gateway to the West, St. Louis.

November in Washington D.C.

The guards are friendly when you walk
at night up toward the Capitol
standing floodlit
white and shining above
its Roman pillars—
"Good evening, where you folks from?"
"Ah, St. Louis, we live there." "Faan-TAS-tic!"—
there's an interruption,
a siren and a flashing cop-car swirling up
through the parking lot behind two lost
cars filled with tourist families,
or maybe terrorists—
but then the cars stop, the cop's lights
quit flashing, there's a friendly
parley and they swing around
and drive out down the street,
and the young friendly guard, mustached,
in black gloves and overcoat, pounds
his hands and says again "FanTASTic" in a way
that means he's checked us out,
so we walk on, around the Capitol
and down dark steps and sidewalk to
the Reflecting Pool—
it must be several acres of still
shimmering dark alive
with streetlights, brilliant green
and red of traffic signals, tail-lights' red glare,
and then from its other side we see
the white unreal dome of the Capitol
pointing down, down, at a star glittering
deep in the pool below it, a very bright
star, Venus we think—at this moment
this most powerful building in the world's
asleep in Xanadu

(*a little water clears it of its deeds,*)
a pleasure-dome where people
—Chinese? Japanese? set up their cameras now
to capture pool and Capitol in one silver shot.
We could walk further, down the Mall,
and past the National Gallery where
they've captured Veronese's paintings for a time.
—Or by the Space Museum, where astronauts
are dummies in their capsules and
sleek missile-launchers stand like Michaels, waiting
to stop time for us
(*they also served*)—
or past the Smithsonian where, I'm told,
the symbols of our Osage people wait, that let us
come down from the stars
and form a nation, here.
Instead, the night being damp, we turn
to walk on back along East Capitol, past
trash receptacles on whose dull orange,
painted in yellow profile, is a REDSKIN—
RE-LOCATED from the BUFFALO NICKEL—
and now **PRESIDENT** over
the old news of this 1988 election, as we
walk eastward, into an orange moon.

Where to Hang Them

Between the hot bath, where the Senator
simmers with his secretary,
and the green ground-pecker at the well,
there runs the buried steel
gaspipe that transforms a ballot box
to cornucopia—but
who drilled the well, who
dug the ditch and laid the pipe, who filled
the ballot box with power and wealth and servants?
The people who are stuck with taxes that
their Senators have voted,
who pay the interest rates that bankers
tell them are needed to combat inflation:
they did all this.
We borrow too much, Mister Volcker tells us, puffing
cigars. We ought to be
like him, and borrow millions.
Hell, the more you borrow, the more
you make, because the less
the interest rates.
The goddamned rich, they know the way.
They raise the interest rates, so they
make more. The people pay the interest rates, so they
have less. And how can the politicians lose? They vote
to raise their salaries when needed. They
have the staff to write their speeches, stuff
their envelopes,
make their reservations, meet constituents, research
the issues and to poll their districts, hold
fund-raisers, so they're re-elected every time. You go
to Washington D.C. and look around.
By God you'll be amazed. Rome hasn't fallen.
Walk through the White House, see the kind of mansion
we give our Emperor, pictures that glorify

our rulers and their wives we hang
up on those walls. Look at the rare
woods, the costly rugs and hangings, look at the guards
at night in cubicles lit by infra-red.
Sit on a park bench just across the street and look
at the floodlit White House with
its dark and empty windows that guards patrol.
Look at the blocks of heavy Federal buildings that
surround it, see
how they post their Doric columns at the top,
not holding up the building but announcing that
we are imperial. For miles around
the bureaucrats are burning
the midnight oil, watchfires of
a hundred circling camps that look down
on the redlight district where one
adult movie festers next door to a
granite-columned brokerage house where furtive men
in raincoats walk past shamed
as pinstriped international bankers make a killing.
The place to hang our rulers' portraits
is on post office walls.

The Readie and Easie Way

for Tom McGrath

—Poets? aaah, hell! you bleeping lingo-dancers, LOOK
how those hyena fictioneers have snatched
out of our Muse her bloody
backbone, story; how flack-jackals mouth
her ribs and jawbones for their rhymes
to slay the Philistines, how ad-vampires tap
blue puns and pulsing metaphors
to puff light beer or heavy tanks, and how
the many-headed media skin the scandals from
her private parts while magpie journals jangle
the remnant jester-bells
at kings or presidents.
Naah, poetry
can't rhyme a rat to death these days, she choked
when Wordsworth, dammit, stuffed
the ME-ME-ME into her larynx so if she moves,
she moves like a squeaky mummy, sobbing
that only Doctor Freud and his
Critic Friends can Understand.
Kindest non-cut of all, pre-carious
towers of ivory seal her sibylline
decay within, phosphorescing
in tenured darkness so no orthodoctor
need certify her false: gwacious, what
a sharp satiwic bite you've got, pwofessor!
Meanwhile, back at the Logos,
those pig-teat Falwells, power-sucking
George Wills, sabertooth-rattling Phyllis
Schlaflys—yes, the names change fast—are out there raising hell
and contributions even as mingy poets
write applications to the corporations begging
meal-money to sit up in a garret
and garrulize. So what's to do?

Maybe
it's time to take back what's
been lost: climb on the air,
juke into journalism,
reach down the tube with rap—just
don't let them call us poets, that's
the cotton wool for zircons: NO PEDESTAL
BUT A COLUMN! Rise up! Jehoshaphat into
new bones and guts and brains, speak again
in that voice which by God draws
plutonium tears down plutocratic cheeks:
come preach, come prophesy, come roll them in
the aisles with comedy and tongues
of fire; metamorphose the maggotheaded
majoritarians right and left, kick
their covert-action terrorists right
where their conscience ought to be! Hell,
write NOVELS if you can't do better! just
try not to turn into some prosing
fictioneer, fluffing
the reader's pillow one more time. . . .
Come ON, you lousy lamprey-breaths—
do you want to live
FOREVER?

A Cardinal, New Snow, and Some Firewood

Once when I was getting firewood down by Buck Creek I had a long talk with a cardinal who was wintering there. Of course I don't understand the summer language of cardinals, the kind you hear when green things come back. That isn't meant for us but for themselves, and all I can make out is that it has to do with love and war. I've stood and listened, looking up through the white locust blossoms at the blue sky, in all that fragrance and new bright green, and a scarlet flash singing there, but it was just birdsong, it hid the meaning like a nest someplace away from where it sang. Finding it would probably kill it anyhow.

But in winter, when there is new snow, and snow-lined branches in a blue sky, and the crimson flashes down to a bush for coral berries or a wild rose-hip, sometimes if you're sitting quietly near it will talk. And their winter language is like the new snow, I can read it for a while, until it gets tracked all over with human things that come out of me and walk around as if it was their back yard. Down by Buck Creek early that morning, I saw it up in a huge American elm, then it dropped from sight into a holly below, then flew back up into a tendrilly mass of grapevine in the elm's branches, swaying a little when the wind would pull at the tree's upper boughs. The woods were almost silent, and the wind did not come down among the blackberry patches and undergrowth except to put a finger down the back of my neck and whisper from dead weeds behind me. The inch of new snow had fallen after midnight and in this early light shadow-lines were sharp across it. I brushed off snow to sit on a stump, and saw going past the stump a weasel's tracks. The snow told me where it had lunged after a cottontail, and where the rabbit jumped and veered and got away, and the weasel had chased it, stopped, sat up, turned, dived into the big brushpile left by woodcutters alongside a tangle of blackberry vines. It was while I was reading that part of the past that the cardinal sang.

"The weasel isn't there, he's down by the creek. He found a covey of bobwhites and killed two," the cardinal said.

When I looked up to where he was singing, he was perched on the lowest branching of the long grapevine. I knew he was talking to me.

He was looking at me first with one eye, then the other. I answered him out loud before I thought.

"I guess weasels have to live," I said. When I spoke the place went completely quiet. I had thought there was no sound, but when I spoke time stopped breathing for a heartbeat and I wondered if I was delirious. It felt like that, everything recognizable but different, changed the way sound is changed under water.

"You don't have to talk," the cardinal said. "The snow is inside you and I can see what you say walking there. When you speak out, the sound tramples around and all the meanings that are friendly go into hiding and the others start sniffing for me."

I looked at him swaying on the grapevine thirty feet from the ground, and I looked on up into the great leafless elm with snow fluffs along some branches still, and into blue sky where a jet-trail was drawing itself thin and straight out of nowhere, fluffing out behind like the rattles of an invisible snake.

"It's the President's plane," the cardinal said. "Lots of reporters up there, but he's in the private parts of the plane talking about how to keep a scandal dark, while they're up there trying to see what each other is going to write about next."

I looked at the cardinal's black mask just as a pat of snow, dislodged by the wind-sway, came down in sparkling crystals. For a second he was looking at me with his beak open and I saw an old face surrounded by a ruff of diamonds.

"The President is looking out his window," he said. "He sees a snowy landscape with not a soul in view. We know he is there, he doesn't know we are here; it has to do with power. At one time he was a weasel on a high branch swaying in the wind, furious that the squirrel had jumped to another tree. Now he is fullbellied, blind, warm, feels safe. His titanium cocoon has translucent spots for him to look through. A flock of swans could bring him down, but we won't do that. Less harm this way."

"I must be dreaming," I said.

"Why? What do you think a dream is, anyhow?"

"Something a mind makes up when it's sleeping."

"What does a mind make up when it's waking?"

"That's not making up things."

"What makes you think that?"

"Because there are others hearing and seeing the same things."

"You mean I'm not a red bird, an other, I'm just you?"

"I made you up somehow."

"And the President, and the weasel that isn't there but left its tracks, you made them up. You made the snow up. My voice, you're making it up. I haven't told you anything, then."

"That's right."

"And someone made you up as well as me?"

"Of course. But not just one person . He, and all the people reading these words. They made me up, a lot of different me's according to their minds. They made me up, they're looking at me, hearing me. The snow is in their minds. These words are tracks in the snow."

"Sure," the cardinal said. "You know that new snow is a wonderful computer. You can retrieve history from it, all the living beings who have moved across it. Water forgets, snow remembers. Have you any idea how many kinds of snow there are? The spread of white blossoms, say, in April and May, they remember. They record what bees are doing, and the trees remember it in August and you taste it as apricots, apples, plums. I can retrieve tiny variations in air pressure from June, and return them as song in December. You can retrieve from stone the consonants of Babylon. Greenland remembers, ten thousand feet down in its ice, the volcanoes of Java, the fireflies from space, of a hundred thousand years ago."

There was a flash of dark wings, a swerving and fan-tailed slewing around the elm's huge trunk toward the crimson bird on its grapevine, a curved beak open, talons stretching. The redbird launched sharply down towards me, the hawk close behind. I heard a hard fierce voice say get out of its way, but I stood up just as the cardinal dodged around and behind me, then claws grappled suddenly, my cap flew off, the flurry passed and when I turned, scarlet flashed into the holly-tree, the Cooper's hawk banked past its spiky green darkness, hovered briefly on beating wings, and went coursing away into darker woods toward Buck Creek.

"Son of a bitch," the voice said faintly, "those politicians may not be so dumb as I thought." Then it was silent.

I walked on over to cordwood we had stacked the week before, and stamped and waited till they came with the pickup. I was thinking how the cut wood remembers years of sunlight, then lets go in snapping, sighing light and warmth from the ashes. What the red coals say, I was thinking, I'll have to listen to. What the words release, I leave to those who read. Some of it lived there ten thousand years ago, some never was. Across the snowy pages dark words leap and sway. A red bird is singing in them. What year, what year? he sings. This one, this one, this one, they answer. Blossom, blossom, blossom, he sings. And they do.

I

We of the Osage Nation have come,
as the Naming Ceremony says,
down from the stars.
We sent ahead
our messengers to learn
how to make our bodies,
to make ourselves a nation,
find power to live, to go on,
to move as the sun rises and never fails
to cross the sky into the west
and go down in beauty into the night,
joining the stars once more
to move serenely across the skies
and rise again at dawn, letting
the two great shafts of light beside the sun
become white eagle plumes in the hair
of children as we give their names.

When we came down, our messengers
encountered beings
who let us take their bodies
with which we live into the peaceful days;
we met the Thunder, and the Mountain Lion,
the Red Bird, and the Cedar Tree,
Black Bear, and Golden Eagle.
As eagles, we came down,
and on the red oak tops
we rested, shaking loose with our weight
great showers of acorns, seeds
for new oaks, and our daily bread.

The leaves were light and dancing and
we saw, through the trees,

the sun caught
among leaves moving
around its light; it was
the leaves, we saw,
those light beings, who raised
as they danced the heavy
oak-trunks out of earth,
who gathered the wind and sunlight,
the dew and morning into timbered
lodges for the sun and stars.

And so of course, we sang:
Nothing's lighter than leaves, we sang,
ghost-dancing on the oak tree as the spirit moves,
and nothing heavier than the great
sun-wombing red oaks which their dancing
in time has raised up from this earth where we
came down as eagles.
It will not end, we sang,
in time our leaves of paper will
be dancing lightly, making a nation of
the sun and other stars.

2

Coming down to Las Vegas as
a passenger on Frontier Airlines is
a myth of another color. At the Stardust Inn deep
within that city of dice and vice and Warhead Testing,
I was to give a paper
to the Rocky Mountain Modern Language Association
on Trickster Tales.
I gave it, and
I got out solvent, astonished,
and all but stellified
on wings of flame, like Elijah
or Geoffrey Chaucer in *The House of Fame*, up
up into the stars above Lake Mead, and I looked down

into its twinkling heaven
and thought back to the many-splendored
neon and krypton lights of Las Vegas
that throbbed with the great lake's power;
I remembered the dead rapids and waterfalls
drowned in Glen Canyon and Lake Mead,
thought of those bodies of
water, swollen so huge that earth itself
quivers with constant
small tremors from them—
and there looking up at me with
his Las Vegas eyeball was the Trickster Monster,
flashing with lightning from his
serpents of copper lifted up on crossbars—
but then I remembered how
among the streaked and painted bluffs that surround
Las Vegas I saw the October dawn come streaked
and painted down from the eastern skies to brighten
the walk from my Travelodge over the street
to a vacant lot under
its desert willows
where lived a wren, some vivid orange flowers
papery on thornleaved stems hugging the sand,
and one empty billfold
with its credit cards spread around a sole
identity card that pictured
a security guard from San Diego,
the naval base there.
I turned the billfold in
to the motel clerk, the wren
pleaded innocent and flew away like me,
and when I got the orange flower
back to St. Louis and put it in
a glass of water, it turned the water
to pungent amber and wilted as if
I'd killed it with kindness.
—That Trickster, he always carries

lost identity cards and desert flowers
and finds himself
surrounded by dawn.

And so I sang
how the white sails of Columbus, of
Cortez and the Pilgrims brought
this krypton iris here and made
the desert bloom,
how they raised
the great light-sculptured houses
of cards and dice on sand;
I sang how
the rainbow ghosts of waterfalls
are pulsed into the sockets of
Las Vegas light flashing in crimson green
gold and violet its humongous word,
VACANCY,
VACANCY,
up to the dancing stars.

As Brer Coyote Said,

the country's
not quite all field
or fence, blackberries root
wild on stony soil
among scrub timber, their
thorn-vines still there in winter as the booted feet thrash
through hip-high hay, brown and stemmy, after
the dogs and rabbits running blind
to blackberry briars until they've
grabbed and torn saying
this ground is taken for the smaller nations who live
BENEATH, who perch BETWEEN—
surviving too spring's burnings with the wind swinging
its gold-crackling scythe across
the meadow purging
old nests and vines among rock-croppings
as dried cow-chips go smoking
back to the sky or floating
creekwards with rains and leave
the marginal things such black clarity to grow in, wild
plums whiten, chokecherries bloom
along winding gullies,
new shoots spring green and fork
the air like snaketongues coming out
of eggs to flicker tasting—
the vines flower loosely
when sunburn days move in
and bare feet grow tough enough to walk
among thorn fringes on the way
down to the low-water bridge
(the rock-riffles and pool darkshining
under arch of elms like a water-floored
cathedral,
brown naked bodies poise,

fly on the ropeswing down
from their high bank and skim
with one heel and rise up, up,
to drop through topwater's warmth into brown
darkness of spring-cold upwellings like waving
tendrils around the thighs)—
and July,
July is **BERRIES**—
the heaping pans
and handled buckets spilling their black shining
with some a tight
red still
and reaching fingers, even stung
by a hidden wasp to swell
like soft cucumbers, are consoled
by cobblers, whose thick doughs and crusts purple
with juice and flake with sugar under yellow spill
of Jersey cream into blackpurple berries that taste
like nothing else
waiting in roadside ditches,
rockpiles, woodmargins,
FREE
between their thorns.

An Eagle Nation

For the Camp/Jump brigades

You see, I remember this little Ponca woman
who turned her back to the wall and placed her palms
up over her shoulders flat on the wall
and bent over backwards and walked her hands down the wall
and placed them flat on the floor behind her back—that's
how limber she was, Aunt Jewell,
when I was a boy.
And FAST! you wouldn't BELIEVE how she could sprint:
when an Osage couple married, they would ask Aunt Jewell
to run for the horses for them.
Now she's the eldest in her clan, but still the fastest
to bring the right word, Ponca or English, sacred or
profane, whatever's needed to survive she brings it, sometimes in
a wheelchair, since her heart
alarms the doctors now and then.
So one bright day we loaded
the wheelchair, and ourselves, and lots of chicken
barbecued and picnic stuff
into our cars and zoomed away
from Ponca City and White Eagle, *Southward Ho!*
To the Zoo, we said, the Oke City Zoo—we'd picnic there!
Grandchildren, see, they love the zoo,
and has she got GRANDchildren? well, maybe
one of her children knows how many, the rest of us
stopped counting years ago, so there were quite a few
with serious thoughts of chicken barbecue and we all rolled in
to the Zoo and parked, and we walked, and scrambled, and rolled,
we scuttled and sprinted, we used up all the verbs
in English, she'd have to get those Ponca words
to tell you how we made our way,
but somehow we ALL of us got in, and found
the picnic tables, and we feasted there and laughed
until it was time to inspect the premises, to see just what
the children of Columbus had prepared for us.

Snow leopards and black jaguars, seals and dolphins, monkeys and
baboons, the elephants and tigers looked away
thinking of Africa, of Rome, oceans, dinnertime, whatever—
and as for us, we went in all directions,
grandchildren rolled and bounced like marbles up and down
the curving asphalt ways, played hide and seek, called me to look
at camels maybe. And then we were all
getting tired and trying to reassemble, when Casey
came striding back to where we were wheeling Aunt Jewell
and said "Mom,
there's this eagle over here you should see,"
and we could tell it mattered. So we wheeled along
to this cage set off to itself with a bald eagle sitting,
eyes closed and statue-still,
on the higher perch inside, and there was a couple
standing up next to the cage and trying
to get its attention.
A nice white couple, youngish, the man
neatly mustached and balding, the woman
white-bloused and blondish: the man clapped hands
and clicked his tongue and squeaked, and whistled. The eagle
was motionless. Casey wheeled Aunt Jewell
a little to the side. The man stopped making noises.
He and the woman looked at each other, then at us, and
looked away.
There was a placard on the cage's side that said:
This bald eagle was found wounded, and
although its life was saved, it will never fly again,
so it is given this cage to itself.
Please do not feed him.
Aunt Jewell, from her wheelchair, spoke in Ponca to him,
so quietly that I could hardly hear
the sentences she spoke.
Since I know only
a few words of Ponca, I can't be sure
what she said or asked, but I caught the word
Kahgay:
Brother, she said.

The eagle opened his eyes and turned his head.
She said something else. He partly opened his beak
and crouched and looked head-on toward her,
and made a low shrill sound.
The white couple were kind of dazed, and so was I.
I knew she was saying good things for us.
I knew he'd pass them on.
She talked a little more, apologizing
for all of us, I think.
She put one hand up to her eyes and closed them for a while
till Casey handed her a handkerchief,
and she wiped her eyes.
"I guess we're 'bout ready to go now," Aunt Jewell said,
so we wheeled along back to the car, and we gathered all
the clan and climbed aboard
and drove from the Zoo downtown to where
the huge *Red Earth* powwow was going on, because
her grandson Wesley, Mikasi, was dancing there.
We hadn't thought Aunt Jewell's heart
was up to Zoo and Powwow in one day, but as usual she
knew better. They CHARGED ADMISSION, and that really
outraged my Ponca folks, for whom
a powwow should be free. Worse than that,
the contest DANCERS had to pay a fee.
"That's not our way," Aunt Jewell said.
But once inside we found our way,
wheelchair and all, up to the higher tiers,
where we and thousands of Indian people looked down
to the huge Arena floor where twelve drums
thundered and fourteen hundred dancers spun and eddied round,
and dancing in his wolfskin there
was Mikasi where Casey pointed, and we saw
his Grampa Paul Roughface gliding
with that eagle's calm he has,
and I saw how happy Casey and Mike were then
that their eldest son was dancing down there, and I felt
what the drum did for Aunt Jewell's heart and ours, and she told us
of seventy years ago when she was a little girl and her folks

would load the wagons up there in White Eagle and go
and ford the Arkansas into the Osage country and drive all day
and camp at night on the prairie and then drive on
to the Grayhorse Osage Dances, or those in Pawhuska even.
I remembered how Uncle Woody Camp had told me
of going to the Osage dances later and seeing her
for the first time and asking:
"Who IS that beautiful Ponca girl over there?"
and someone said,
"Oh that's McDonald's girl,"
and they met that way.
And he and Uncle Dwain would tell
of the covered wagon in which they rode,
my Irish and Scotch-Irish mother's folks, from Missouri out
to the Kansas wheat harvest, and then on down
to the Osage Reservation in Oklahoma, where mules were needed,
and our grandfather hauled the bricks to build
the oil-boom Agency town of Pawhuska, where the million-dollar
lease sales, and the Osage Dances, were held.
So I was thinking how the eagles soared,
in their long migration flights, over all these places,
how they looked down on the wagons moving
westward from Missouri, eastward from Ponca lands
to meet in Pawhuska, how all the circles
had brought us into this Oklahoma time and what
had passed between cage and wheelchair before
we mounted up to view on this huge alien floor the long-ago drum
in its swirling rainbow of feathers and
bells and moccasins lifting up here
the songs and prayers from long before cars or wagons,
and how it all has changed and the ways are strange but
the voices still
are singing, the drum-heart
still beating here, so whatever the placards on
their iron cages may have to say, we the people,
as Aunt Jewell and Sun Dancers say,
are an **EAGLE NATION**, now.

What the Eagle Fan Says

*For Bob and Evelyne Voelker, Dale and Arlene Besse,
and the St. Louis Gourd Dancers*

I strung dazzling thrones   of thunder beings
on a spiraling thread   of spinning flight,
beading dawn's blood   and blue of noon
to the gold and dark   of day's leaving,
circling with Sun   the soaring heaven
over turquoise eyes   of Earth below,
her silver veins,   her sable fur,
heard human relatives   hunting beneath
calling me down,   crying their need
that I bring them closer   to Wakonda's ways,
and I turned from heaven   to help them then.
When the bullet came   it caught my heart,
the hunter's hands   gave earth its blood,
loosened light beings   and let us float
toward the sacred center   of song in the drum,
but fixed us first   firm in tree-heart
that green light-dancers   gave to men's knives,
ash-heart in hiding where   a deer's heart had beat,
and a one-eyed serpent   with silver-straight head
strung tiny rattles   around white softness
in beaded harmonies   of blue and red—
now I move lightly   in a man's left hand,
above dancing feet   follow the sun
around old songs   soaring toward heaven
on human breath,   and I help them rise.

This poem offers thanks for the honor of being given eagle feathers
which were then set into a beaded fan. It tells how the eagle in flight
pierces clouds just as a beadworker's needle goes through beads and
buckskin, spiraling round sky or fan-handle—and how the eagle flies
from dawn to sunset, linking day and night colors as they are linked

35

on a Gourd Dancer's blanket (half crimson, half blue), and as they are linked in the beading of the fan's handle. The poem's form is the alliterative meter used by the Anglo-Saxon tribes, and its mode is the Anglo-Saxon "riddle," in which mysterious names are given to ordinary things: here, tree leaves are *green light-dancers*, wood is *tree-heart* or *ash-heart*, clouds are *thrones of thunder beings*. I hope the one-eyed serpent will find its ordinary name in the reader's memory.

Moccasins for Christophoros

a memorable fancy

So I said: "Would you mind repeating that, Chickadee!"
"Of course," he said. And he did, as you see. If you want to know
more, you can ask him yourself. This is what he said:

The question of the Nobel Prize came up again shortly after the
Gospels, Acts and Epistles were published, and before they got to be
the Literary Canon with footnotes and all the elaborate necessary
explanations. There was a claque voting for Mark as most original—
but Matthew's coterie was outraged by this claim, since their can-
didate offered plenty of stories never told by Mark, and all of them
beautifully phrased and deeply symbolic. However, John's publishers
had votes on the committee, and so did Luke's, and Paul's supporters
also jumped in with the argument that everybody knew "John" and
"Luke" were pen names, and it was strongly suspected that several
people may have collaborated on the works of both so-called authors,
and the Prize Committee was likely to be embarrassed by revela-
tions of plagiarism by those "authors" from famous ancient writers,
Jeremiah for instance, not to mention a lot of anonymous Greeks.

So it looked like an unbreakable impasse, and the publishers were
sitting around glowering at each other. Then an old lady appeared
and said to them, "Listen, my name is Mary and I GAVE most of
these stories anyhow; these guys only wrote them down. What they
didn't get from me they got from my cousin Elizabeth, or her hus-
band Zechariah, if not from the friends my son made, or his enemies
for that matter. Why are you all sitting around here arguing who told
these stories FIRST, anyhow?"

The prize committee gracefully transformed themselves into Nor-
way and went back home, but when Mary turned around she was
looking back down a line of faces, mostly bearded.

"Aunt Mary," she heard one of them say, and saw it was John,
carrying his head in his hand. But once Mary had walked away into
the darkness, smiling and nodding to herself, John turned his head to
look behind him. Elijah stood there waiting for the chariot to come
down. He lifted one hawkwing eyebrow at John.

"Evening, John," Elijah said. "I've had to ask Moses over here to try and settle this committee squabble if he will."

"Ah," Moses said. "Th-th-th-they always tr-tr-try to s-s-s-say I wrote it first. I m-m-m-m- might as well s-s-s-s-send you right away to the p-p-p-p-people these stories f-f-first w-were told by, in the Garden." And there arguing hotly with only their figleaves on were Adam and Eve.

They were pretty serious about which of them should get the Nobel Prize for the fruits of this tree. At first Eve was way ahead on points, but Adam simply put her back into his side and she had to shut up. But then an angel on the prize committee remarked that in his view a compromise award to both was in order. He pulled a wingfeather out and began to write the acceptance speeches for them in rainbow ink. At this point, however, God quietly cleared his throat. The angel exploded into a thunderstorm and God claimed the prize.

"Pretty presumptuous argufying, seeing that I made all of you, not to mention the tree and the garden and the rest of it," he said cheerfully. He held the world up in one hand and looked at Noah and all the astounding creatures bobbing on the Ark inside their bottle. But just as he was going to pour them out into the Near Eastern deserts, a small bearded rabbi tapped him on the shoulder.

"I don't want to be rude, but you give me no choice," the man said gently. And God shrugged and sank back down into Ur of the Chaldees, leaving the Prize Book fluttering there. The bearded man plucked it from the air and closing his eyes devoutly began reciting its words. On the page, stars shone terribly in a great darkness, a whirlwind spun them into the Milky Way and poured it into the great Sea of Brass in the Temple. But when the rabbi opened his eyes, his grandmother from Chaldea had come to collect what he owed her. He nodded respectfully, handed over the Prize Book and sat down among the potsherds, closing his eyes again. Around his silence a hurricane was composing psalms of praise.

His grandmother stood there holding the prize gingerly. "As if he thought those stories were all made up by him," she said. "Well, maybe I ought to step over and find out what those Osages might trade for this. That was a gorgeous buffalo story they decorated just before they moved to Oklahoma."

When she looked around, the buffalo was walking alongside her.

"Granddaughter," he said, "you're always generous, but sometimes even you remember less than there is. Your sister told me you'd be coming. Thank you for your story."

"Oh, you're welcome, grandfather. So you made us up, I guess. Now I'd better go back. This is a nice place here in Oklahoma. You come visit us in Eden. We have our dances there in summer."

"We remember them, granddaughter. You know our Sun Dance Songs still have cousins there. You take this buffalo robe back with you now. It has the sunrise here, the sunset there, the noonday at its center. Wrap it around your children when they sleep."

"I will. And when you come to dance with us, maybe there'll be a robe of stars to bring back to this tallgrass prairie for the people."

When she had gone the buffalo stood quietly looking down at a worn brown sandstone by the water's edge.

"Thank you, grandson," the stone said. "It's a great story, and I appreciate your giving it to me at this dance. I want to say how good it makes our people feel that you would give us this story. We want you to know that because we have always been treated well by you and your people and because we have always had a good heart and good feelings for you and your family, we will always welcome you when you come to see us. We will be honored when you come to visit. We want you to know you can come to stay with us any time, all we have will be there for you any time you come and see us."

When the buffalo had gone the Sun rose and spoke very clearly to the stone.

"Thank you, grandchild, for that story. I heard the water singing with you, and the wind dancing, and the grass and trees making the tremolo with them. The Moon and the Stars and I want to say we appreciate the honor you are giving us here. We know it is always good to come and visit our relatives here. You have feasted us and we have danced with you and heard all these songs and stories. We feel at home here, we want you to feel at home whenever you come and see us, and you are always welcome to come any time. When we see these things you give us, when we wear them and use them, we will think of you and our hearts will have good thoughts for you and your family and your people. We know we will move sometimes in other roads but our ways will always bring us together, that's how our circles are. We will be going home now, but we will be seeing you in our home or in your home."

"Well," the darkness said. "So you've come back, grandchildren. These are beautiful stories you have been given. They fit you just right, almost. You can rest here for a while and let me adjust them just a little. Your grandfather and I will have a word or two about them while you eat. You can say hello to Mary over there, and Paul down here, and Crazy Horse. They'll be happy to hear again from Stone and Sun. And Mohammed talking here with Abraham and Moses and Confucius and Emily Dickinson. You see she has them wondering again about her dog Buddha. She says he wants a prairie, but one clover and a bee will do. He already has the reverie-beads."

So that, said Chickadee, is how I heard the story of these stories. They didn't seem to mind my listening to all of it. I promised to bring the leaves and flowers north if they let me listen—so here they are.

"Thank you, Chickadee," I said.

Homework at Oxford

—It's probably because we were always trying
to have enough money to eat
that I can taste and smell the truckloads
of summer that came by and sometimes
turned jouncing up the long
dirt lane from U.S. Sixty to our house—
they saw kids swarming out in the yard,
white house with a green roof and a big white
two-story garage, haybarn and cowbarn,
nothing around but meadow, no crops, no
rows of corn or hills of watermelons, a lot of hungry kids
that would be wanting what they were taking round
from their truck farms or orchards—
elephantine loads of melons, sometimes the light
green long ones, the striped ones, the dark
green cannonballs, incredible abundance,
or old swaying trucks loaded with bushels of peaches,
apples and apricots, of grapes, of pears that I
remember. Where had they come from,
that's what I wonder now—
over in Sand Creek Valley by the little town
in the Osage hills, the hamlet really,
they called it Okesa where we
drove once; there we saw a hillside full
of orchards, berry bushes, the sandy bottomland shaggy
with watermelon vines where the great green melons rounded
heavy and warm on the loam—
it struck me staring from the car, how strange
that dirt does turn into their sweet crisp red flesh
and juice in the mouth, that those long vines
can draw the dark earth up and make it melons, and I said
to myself, how does the seed know to make
a watermelon and not an apricot? Then we had brought

our dimes and pennies for a summer's day, we took
the silver and the copper and we turned
them into two huge melons that the blond boy went casually out
into the field and pulled, just those we wanted,
he took our thirty cents and we—
I think we drove away back down to Sand Creek and in
the pebbly shallow ford we drove out in the water and killed
the engine and we took
the melons from the trunk and in the shallow ripples splashed
each other and the car, we washed the car, the melons,
we took them out onto the bank and sat
on a blanket spread across the grass and stuck
a great long butcher knife into the first green melon and it split,
it was so ripe it cracked almost before the knife
could cut it open, the red heart
looked sugar-frosted, dewy with juice and the pieces
broke to our fingers better than to knives,
in the mouth crisp and melting fragrant, spicy nearly,
as pieces of rind were scattered the ants reporting mountains
of manna climbed and swarmed and buried themselves
in our leavings
as we stripped to shorts and underthings and waded
down into the deeper colder pool below the ford
where the springs welled slowly out from under the bouldery bank
at the bend, and swimming I thought,
now the melon is turning into me, and my sisters and brothers,
my mother and
father and uncles and aunts and into the
ants feasting there on the melon-rinds,
and into the grass and the trees growing there,
and into the dirt—
and Sand Creek is turning, this day is turning to
night, so now when we go home I'll remember and it
will be turned into words, and maybe sometime
it would all grow again a long way off, a long way into
the future, and that's what a few pennies and dimes can do

if you have them, a few seeds, a little rain where creekwaters
rise, and the whole world
turns into food for all
the different beings in their times.

October, Isle of Skye

Wading up Brunigill's rush
for a long time is a question
of where to place each boot
on a rock that will hold, advance;
of not slipping on moss-slime's
green blackness under the swashing
of water past boots—
then eyes raise to a pool
too golden-deep for boots,
and before climbing around it, pause
and stretch and look down through
amber lucence where
slow gold-lit ripplings touch
white crystals in rockbed,
till a rowan-berry comes bobbing,
red-round and lightly,
to ride through the pool—
then boots go up over sheep-paths
to the heathery ridge and
a bumblebee knee-brushed from
purple paper-firm bells
drops wet and stunned,
chill mist on her wings,
tumbles in browning blossoms
and on her back caught
in the jungle of heather her front legs
rise drowned and waking, hook
slowly a heather-twig, pull
the fur-body up as antennae wag
through green and amber sensing
late pollen, nectar
for bee-bread in burrows—
and light changes dazzling
in downstreaming mist,

blue brilliance,
cloudrush,
soft greyblue
sunfilled,
while newlit water
birdshrills and gurgles,
and down again climbing
bootplace by bootplace
to the stream and
its rowanberry raft
by moss-edge of pool—
that from scarlet seed
over amber movement
a green tree may sway.

Separated from friends
still climbing that gorge
with its dripping moss
and red-orange slimes,
here tracing the stream up
over this edge through
bronze grasses shaking
in mist pouring down
from the taut ridgeline,
trailing its damp fringes
overhead and touching cool
breath into face:
climb now toward the delicate
last waterfall shivering
from its flat rock-shelf just
under the mist that
veils the peak;
here where spattering drops down bare
rock, the stream ducks
into turf green and sheepcropped,
tankling in echoes under
my boots climbing up to the rock
bared by its waterfall—
spreadeagling up it with rubber
soles uncertain on slime-slips
and fingers sliding on shifting
boulders loose-poised to drop and I'm
slipping spread out sliding
toward cold splashing on face and down
my crotch! till I catch and haul back
up cold-balled to foothold and
firm handgrip, kneeing careful up—
waterswashed, teeter back, forward,
over! on top from bent waist up as

hands scrabble slime-slick rock—
sprawled full-length now in
slick swift water, push slowly
up from fingertips to stand turning
at the edge,
                looking down to
figures climbing small over
lip of gorge in the russet
bracken: Maud waves, I point up
to mist-hung peak, turn toward
it, climb a honeybronze knoll over
heatherclumps, springy through the
bog-squish under next ledge where deep
lush mosses plush, claret on primrose,
a ruby throne set shaky in citron carpet,
boulders brilliant with tangerine, umber,
bluegray luminous lichens; star-moss
springy under boots; a roar
of red grouse bursting
(two of them) and slanting up the green
turfline and
            gone over ridge,
omen for climbing now? running
uphill with heart beating like
the grousewings, to pause at shelf's
edge and look back where friends took
the other stream-rift, mist
rising between us and they
disappear into its folds—
peak left for me now.
Slanting left and right up its steep,
past sheepdroppings,
            waterdrools,
cropped green turf loose over
stones, I walk out to rest
on the next shelf's edge, windpushed

see through sudden mist-door down to
terraced slides over ocean,
pale gold and green rectangles with
haystacks in the dale's
cupped hand gentle and small, the white
sunlit houses far under great brown
meltings of bog and heather, pools
like snakes silvering terraces where
far down two rocks rise up and
wave, from bank above stream there—
I wave back thinking may have
imagined in that grey mauve
haze, Frankie and Joe—and I turn to
the last slope, spiraling up steep
with legs and wind going noisy,
cloud swooping and beating
hood into cheeks; pushing
with hands against thighs exhausted,
leaning forward, scrambling
up a last few rocks through cataracts of
wind, come panting out on
the top—
the brown grass spreading
its flat firm footing and a gale buffeting
face, I walk head-down with flapping
hood up a three-foot knoll to look
south into mist-roilings that circle a
sundazzle drifting toward me, think
drytongued of the tumbling stream
below, and walking into surfing wind
stop by unruffled pool shivering with light
under dark peat-bank, step
out over soft quaking peninsula and
stretch prone on hands deep in lemon
moss-rough, touch mouth to water, sip
live coldness in belly as mist

breaks open to a flare of
sun through windrush; I rise and
march briskly windhurried back to
peak-rim and see
shadow and sunlight sweeping over
Dunvegan Castle washed by a sunpatch
gleaming far out on the greysilk loch,
whitecaps out farther,
rain darkens over the right distance,
leftwards sun is brilliant on the
amethyst and emerald windpaths over
to dark-mountained Uist where the
white clouds hang misty along
its blue slopes—
if there were further
to climb here I'd go up gladly, heart
beating faster time, up to the
clear pools between Skye and sky, see
on each knoll climbed what lives
and moves and has its being
all down the bright morning streams from
peak to the sea; but this
is all the top there is, new mist is
rolling in and my dryness filled
with the freshened pool; time
to climb down into the scene with
friends again, see if Joe's pack has
salt and one boiled egg or even
an orange—
though none could taste
like that coming up, when we sat,
after climbing the steep bank, out
on the fifty-foot waterfall's ledge,
under the bright red berries of
a rowan-tree leaning outward, in the
brilliant sun peeling one orange
among us and sharing segments bursting

tart globules on tongues that were
centaurs galloping naked in a driving
orange rain, before this last
peak gathered the clouds around him and
started his play with sun and
rain, up here where I move to start
back down with the mist,
with the wind-lashed rain,
with the weight of my fortieth year, now
driving me, helping me,
down.

"But Still in Israel's Paths They Shine"

Six hundred dark feet the cliffs
from the crash of Atlantic swells
beetle up over their surf
and its patches of seaweed tangling
the waves' drive shoreward
pulsed by the miles-off gray of storms
into this sunlit scene, to
us seated on green headland
with slow-grazing sheep dotted whitely along
gentle slopes to the lighthouse
looking across that wave-thrash at blurred
rock-bands and strata holding each
a million years of sleet and blossoms crushed
to a band of brown; to
us thinking how
down on that shingle walking
we saw this morning the million
pebbles brought down from the cliffs' monochrome to lie
all streaked and dappled, spotted and milky and veined,
not one like another but all
rounded and smoothly
rubbing together in wetness; us
remembering how
down in the tidal pool's depths by the boulders
a powder-blue jellyfish was pulsing
upward and downward in that bluegreen clearness
as fragile as joy in time
yet riding the Atlantic's power;
us climbing down at noontime all
the way to the stream's mouth where
its last waterfall pours whitely down
to the cove and its peppersalt beach;
us seeing in noon-light how tiny
crab-spiders sidle upon

sand-brilliants and
its grains rough-shaped on palms
as the cliffs where white seabirds soar and
dive,
grains crowding like white
faces in terminal lobbies eroded
by grief and joy, pouring
from the hand like pieces
of broken planets tumbling
and flashing
in space, saying:
the revolution we work for
is revelation and the eyes to see
these shining things and how
they change, and pass,
and are the same.

Letter to Friends on the Isle of Skye

Dear Frankie, Maud, and Joe,
I'm sitting here, sunk
in sloth and St. Louis, and even though
last night when I was walking
a yellow blinking light
spread gold on the rain-glazed street
ahead of me and behind,
its only word was *Caution!* so I keep thinking how
on the Isle of Skye the golden
eagles came down, where Joe
and I were standing on
the waterfall's edge to see the stream
slip glinting down its green vale that quivered
like a wineglass half-filled with purple
ocean, and I was watching
the brown quick wren below us bobbing
into crevices among
great mossy boulders of
the pyramid island beneath
the fall; popping out
through heather-fringe and sending
her silver needle-trill
through swash and champagne thunder,
then pouncing neatly
on pillbugs in the dust
and darkness of their crevice,
and coming out swallowing, swallowing with
her wings akimbo and her
stub tail tilting, one black
eyebead cocked
towards us watching above—
and leaning over the fall-edge looking down
on the wren's darting
business, my senses

gurgling with plastic silver
music, a sudden flick
of my eye ripped
a trilling free from bird-beak and pinned it down by
my boot, to a rock-jut warbling
its wave-spray flute in the throat
of the waterfall's tuba
and waked in my ears the voices
of birds before sunrise streaming
here from stones, from ripples,
and putting my head
up under a granite slab
as into a seashell's concert heard
the ringing of mockingbird changes on
oboes—mosquitoes—coloraturas over
the cataract's bass viol
grumbling upstream—and turning to see that music
instead saw hanging
ten feet over water
great dark brown bird
his yellow eye watching
us, and the wren,
and the twinkling sea—
and he rose as I turned,
he steered with his
spread tail as heavy
as a Viking ship turning
in the aircurrents
over the stream,
he swung and sailed downwind to leftward
but my voice came back and I said
"Turn around, Joe—binoculars!"
and you remember Joe how you turned
and it scared the piss out of you, so
you nearly fell over seeing
that great glaring head down
and his grappling talons lowered even

as he swung into the wind and rose
again up the cliffside, floated
out over the stream
crossing in silence
above its flashing noise
and finding an updraft
rose higher, floating up shelf by shelf
to the clifftop
and over, being joined in the distance by
two others soaring
high against white clouds
(and quartering off
to hunt down the steep sides
of Lorigill where red grouse
and hares would be hiding in bracken)—
but before they had quite vanished,
plunging out from the rock-juts beneath
their great easy circles
there came two ravens—fleeing
voiceless and panicked, flapping across
with black undulations till nearing
the other clifftops they swung smoothly apart
like boys on rollerskates, with a flourish,
to land among broken rocks,
then looked back and croaked
defiance of great gold bullies,
strutting their elegant blackness and laughter
as though just returned from taking,
back in that wilderness of rocks,
to the prophet Elijah
his daily bread.

It's midnight in a drizzling fog
on Sunset Avenue and we are walking
through the scent of orange blossoms and past
a white camellia blown down or flung by someone
onto rainblack asphalt waiting
for the gray Mercedes sedan to run over
and smash its petals and leave us walking in
the smell of Diesel exhaust with
orange-blossom bouquet.

Where the next blue morning
and the gray Pacific meet
as the Palisades fall away
two sparrowhawks are beating
their tapered wings in place, watching
for jay or chewink to stray too far
from their thorny scrub to get back—
and the female suddenly towers,
her wings half-close and she stoops like
a dropping dagger, but down
the steep slope she rockets past them and turns
again into updraft to the clifftops to hover—
as the jay peers out through thorns,
                  and the lines of white surf whisper in.

The Sixties, I think, were not a TOTAL loss:
Things got a little better for Blacks and Indians,
Standing Bear's kids, or Martin Luther King's—
The money's color counts, in Caesar's Palace.

At Tahoe, we floated out over light blue transparence
and saw below us the wave-lights dancing on firm sand,
Or we splashed ashore and lay on the hot heavy sand
To look up at cool mountains and cool blue sky.

As we walked out, a cluster of children ooing
Round a marshy place parted and let us look down
At a frog being swallowed by a garter-snake, hind legs first,
The frog occasionally croaking as though in despair.

When we left the Sierras behind, eastward from Tahoe,
We came twisting down and down and out into dryness
And southward along the Carson Valley the tires went whining
As the motor fluttered under the airconditioner's wheeze

And trees shrank down into thorny weeds and cactus
That dwindled away as the soil spilled off in the wind
Leaving rocks and ashcrust, we moved between rough upthrusts
Of sandstone and basalt; then off to our left we saw

A slash of rock-choked gully start and go twisting
Where through those dry pebbles a stubborn spring
Oozed its liquid around gray willow roots
And the scar zigzagged greener, grew a dustgreen snake

That slid down into burning green alfalfa depths
In a cobalt sky among lines of Lombardy poplars
And brown bales clustered on a jade-green lushness
As we slowed our speed, turned from the shimmering highway

On a street between houses, grocerystore, gaspumps, movie,
A Legion Hall; and saw, driving past, their indoor swimming pool
Like the desert's heart quivering bluegreen with chlorine. . . .
We hit one slot, in Las Vegas, for fifty cents.

SEED-HEAVEN *n* : 1a: *poetic:* maw of a bird, where seeds (e.g. of pokeweed) are either stripped of their pulp and pass through the digestive system, to be dropped with useful nutrients in soil to sprout and begin·a new life-cycle; OR are ground, macerated, and digested to become part of the bird (hence the later sense developments). 1b: birdsong: that which comes from a bird's throat; seed apotheosized to music. [Seed-heaven's cheerful sermoning where the salmon-dawn leaps—Browning, **Quacksalver's Quickies, 286**] 2: counter-intelligence reports. 3: disinformation: poisonous lies hidden in a carcass of truth. 4: gossip; vicious or unsubstantiated slander. 5: dregs; dreck; crap.

Statement on Energy Policy

It's true we have invented quark-extraction,
and this allows our aiming gravity at will;
it's true also that time
can now be made to flow
backward or forward by

the same process. It may be true as well that
what is happening at the focal point,
the meristem of this process,
creates a future kind of space,
a tiny universe that has

quite different rules. In this, it seems,
whatever one may choose to do or be becomes
at once the case. In short,
we have discovered heaven and
it's in our grasp. However,

the Patent Office has not yet approved and cites
less positive aspects of this invention. First, it
does not generate profit, and
it does make obsolete all present
delivery systems for our nukes. Then,

it will let private citizens do things that only
a chosen few, that is, OUR sort, should be allowed—
fly freely from one country
to any other, spreading diseases
and bankrupting transportation.

Home-heating, auto-making industries will be trashed,
employment shelled, depressions spread worldwide,
sheer anarchy descend.
For these and other reasons,
no one must know of this. . . .

And once again we see
the old royal slammer, Oxford Castle,
and still a jail of blackened stones here
rises over the Cherwell, stagnant
in early light; steel
bars between Them and Us, pigeons between the
rusting bars in windows of
a disused tower preen and stare
down at beer-cans light on lilypads, gilt
aluminum petals among the white plastic
bleach-bottles in the bluegreen scum
gathering, crowding towards the weir purring
under this sidewalk, on whose far side
the water takes its fall and comes out
fresh-looking with three mallard hens
bobbing in the current. The sidewalk
trails beside
its rippling shallows past a torn shirt
sodden on stones next to a
rusting manure-fork in the silt.
Here on the lawn-side, blue spruce burgeons for
some blue tits frisking it
of insects; on the other side, dark pools
where weeping willows trail slow fringes under
steel mesh and barbwire of the jail.
Splitting, the streams
go twining off, the sidewalk turns down leftward
to view the County Council and the Former Old
Rectory, now the Center for Further Education with soft
brown stones facing the gray cement and frail windows of
the Council buildings over a green shack labeled
Cafeteria For The Council Staff; and now
it turns again up
Castle Street and curves past Paradise

House with Morrell's coat-of-arms and rises
to Bonn Square and the monument to soldiers of the
Second Oxfordshire Light Infantry killed in
Her Majesty's Service 1897–8, some of
disease others by mutineers it says in some
place called VGANDA; it
broadens now along Queen
Street where a great green-gray crane on four hydraulic
feet is hoisting on swaying chains the
wooden pallets stacked with concrete blocks, up
to mustached workmen, sideburns under yellow
hardhats ready to build (between the Marks and Spencer
and the Star Jeans Shop) some new
Shoppynge Playce in this *towery branchy city* that I've
walked round and left on stone and asphalt not
a single track, except for this.

Outside in St. Louis

Walking through the door
is easy when it is your home—
but then, how many doors
belong to you? In time,
none,
except the one where it turns dark
and timeless. —But
it keeps us entertained, the sidewalk does,
with lighted windows, spring flowers
and autumn leaves, playthings of children
to walk around, step over—left
at dinner time to go inside to smells of
food and dancing pictures
on television screens; and here,
outside,
the pigeons tilt above me on their way
to find loose grain in a feedstore loft:
two, with
rainbows on their necks, descend to
waddle and peck
at ash-wings in the gutter. What,
I wonder, do they fly through, among, within? Me,
I hear the traffic, step
with caution from the curb—
they, inside the whisper of
a soft St. Louis rain, may hear
the ocean speaking: not just the long swells that lash
Pacific shores, but those that boom
on Hatteras, commune on their
subhuman channels with pigeon minds;
maybe the rumbling of Colorado thunderstorms
forecasts for them this weekend's weather—
even through rainclouds, light is polarized to
brilliantine their way; and though

their way back into everlasting spring's
not lighted up, as for
the tiny migrant warblers who fly the Atlantic non-stop,
by star-maps glittering in the
molecules of their genes, their history
is packed rainproof and portable
in sperm and ova, even
the lodestone that they home with just
a speck of ferrite in their brain—
my God, these rock-doves make
of our crumbs a feast, of our windowsills
their trysting-places, set their pullulating
nests into dark empty places warmed by
our wasted heat:
The Outside is
their home, its door the wind, sidewalks just
angelic parking lots—
So when they do
come spiraling down to sidewalks with
an Aphrodisiac sigh of wings, I hear
as from the chariot they once drew,
Her giggling as
they strut and coo: **She** lets them love it on
the outside of
the street's many doors,
as I remind myself in passing over the hard
daily concrete from our here and now
into some other space and time.

Well, suppose *you* were a blue-point Siamese cat, sleeping in the back of a car, up there on the rear window ledge, and the car stopped beside the road, as it had often done on this vacation trip that you had got dragged along on with the catbox in the car and all, and *you* opened your eyes and yawned—but this time you were in Yellowstone National Park and when you looked through the glass a huge black bear's open muzzle was six inches from your eyes? Wouldn't *you* be momentarily at a loss for suitable syntax? Would your tail ever be sleek and calm again? The surprising thing is that Rasha never developed insomnia when we got back to St. Louis, though she may have been even edgier for the next five years. But she was always high-strung.

I remember though seeing the same facial expression on that German's face driving his tractor in front of us, pulling the huge load of baled hay, not far from Aachen. I could just see his left arm stuck straight out and waving, and I was sick of creeping along behind him with a long line of cars hooting behind me, and I thought he was waving me to come on around him on his left. So I stomped the accelerator on our little Volkswagen bug and zoomed up on his left just as he cut his tractor wheels sharply to turn left across my path. He looked at me just the way the Siamese cat looked at the black bear, although his hair did not stand up like hers. I just managed to turn left inside him and miss the pedestrians on the sidewalk as well as the various traffic signs and such, and I never stopped for international negotiations. At dinner that night in the Rhine village— Kork?—I got out the International Driving rulebook and looked up the section on *Arm Signals*. His signal, I think, didn't mean a right turn but a left, and I explained this to Stella and our kids for future reference. What his words meant I don't know exactly, nor do I want to.

I probably looked very like that once in the high school library when I was fifteen and didn't know the young Girls' Gym Teacher had walked up behind me while I was trying to copy my English essay with a fountain pen that had just blotted the word *geloge-nous*. In those days my vocabulary was limited so all I said, not loud (library rules) but forcefully, was *Shucks!* For some reason then I turned round and I saw what the gym teacher *thought* I had said, and we stared at each other like cat and bear. Her face turned white, then red. Mine was no doubt purple or green. When I graduated she still looked narrow-eyed at me.

But the most philosophic surprise was on the mule's face when we were trying to inveigle him under the electrified fence-wire and the stick we were holding the wire up with broke, and the wire came down on his back, and we never did get the fence repaired, although we did catch the mule the next day. It may be that on later reflection the mule found it comical, but leading characters mustn't suspect they are in a comedy, and at the time the mule took the episode seriously. So did the German tractor driver, and so did I after blotting *gelogenous.* I never asked Rasha's opinion. Her vocabulary was too abstract for the comic genre.

Homework at Oxford

Crouched and shivering, here on the soft blue-velvet sofa,
So mangy with wear it sags from its wooden bones,
Electric fire close to cold knees and chill sweaty feet,
I have read all night, with the curtains drawn, in this black book
Of Meister Eckhart's, filled with images of light and talk
Of emptying mind of all images, journeying deep in the soul's
    darkness
To the sweet fountains of life, light within light in God;
Now the book goes dull, the bleared mind won't focus,
My joints tell me the dawn comes soon, and I should be going
In to the cold bedroom to undress on freezing floors,
Climb on the narrow and wobbly bed and try to sleep.
I watch on the mantel's dark wood where it's propped with books
The frostlit red-and-blue swagger, the sprawl and spikiness
Of casual revelation in my unframed print of Breughel's
Adoration of the Magi: so many things alive as Christ,
Pigeons, rooster, ramshackle thatch of the roof. Were they,
Mother and son, journeying beyond all namable things,
Or were the kings? They kneel, as he laughs and glitters, and high
Over the Christ-child hangs his brilliant star, darting
A sword-ray down that is intercepted, on the ragged thatch,
By the rooster's eye that beams straight down into mine outside
The picture. His comb is like the haloes crowning the heads
Of Mary and Joseph, but bloodred as they are gold; his eye
Both shrewd and curious. I rise and stretch, put the dark book back
On its shelf, walk out the door and click over the dim
Concrete hall, down three steps to the college gardens.
Chill here, dark, a little breeze from the east. Crunching
Along the gravelled walk on numb feet the jar of earth
Strikes harshly through knee and ankle. The breeze of dawn,
But no light yet. I walk toward the ancient wall and up
Onto the gravelled rampart-walk, then lean my hand and weight
On the soft stone, look out over the darkness of Merton Meadows.
I hear the sighs of cattle bedded in the lush grass.

A few move now; now one heaves twice, and is standing,
Coughs up its cud; I hear the jaws calmly chewing.
Another cow stands up, I hear how its tongue laps out
And encircles grass, pressed against lower teeth, the ponderous
Head yanks, and grass with a tiny shriek gives way; I know
The muffled drooling grind of teeth, long swallowing throbs.
I hold my face to the herd, testing for warmth on eyes
And forehead: only the smell of hot grass, bodies, manure,
The ghost of milk; it might be morning darkness in Oklahoma.

We climbed, once, in the dark green grove below the pond,
Up young persimmon trees, tall and slender,
Among their glossy green leaves and brittle limbs
Of a warm September morning when the pond
Would spill a silverlet through red-pebbly clay and down
To the crawdads' pool in a run of clean-gurgling water.
Up high, we looked down on the dam or into its willows,
Tall and sad and lightleaved as mist in the shifting breezes:
A redwinged blackbird would be strutting, high on a dead
    top twig—
Tailspreading and flaunting his epaulettes and honey-creaking,
Till one of us would throw a green persimmon at him:
Hard and aluminum-smooth on the fingertip throwing it flashed
Up out of the grove and clipped through the willows where he
Would take flight at once over the pond to his cattails,
And his darkbrown mate and their friends would parley there
On their swinging stems, and discuss the persimmon situation.
High in our treetops we would start throwing now at each other,
Climbing dangerously out to grasp the heavy clusters,
Balancing to throw yet keep the limb underfoot, and with one hand
Holding some other yielding limb that would never swing right
    in time
With the one underfoot; persimmons bouncing off treetrunks or
Maybe foreheads, and reaching to throw Crack! the limb gone,
    dropping
Through crackle of twigs and branchwhip on hands till a
    strong limb

Flexing had held, had held, and time for the tingling upward look
At the broken limb's fragrance of raw gold, down at the dizzy earth
Till thump! in the chest, persimmons flying again between trees,
A splat and its yowl, warfare stopping at once till the tears
Died down and all agreed not to throw at faces this time
With handfuls new-grabbed and flung shouting, rackets of laughter
And fruit slashing the leaves, swishing down into dry brown grass
—Brown grass—no, from an October morning now in the trees,
Persimmons ripe among bare twigs drop soft on reaching fingers,
Melt sweet-sandy in mouth filling with seeds on quivering tongue
That cleans the slippery seeds of sweetness, spurts them on ground
Through puckered lips, tongue and mouth gone woolly with pucker.
Cold October day that wild ducks lit on the pond as a flight
    of geese
Was circling and passing over in a windy sunbright sky
—Seeing the ducks light we'd slipped down through the meadow
    stubble
The path we'd made to the pond, stooped through the
    barbed-wire fence
Where the wire groaned in its rusty staple as the post wobbled
And Quack! from the pond: when we scrabbled up over the dam
We were just in time to see two pairs of the ducks flap skittering
Across the pond till webs hit waves and they bounced
Into the air with a silken shriek of wings beating in time,
And six feet off the water all in formation they turned
Over the cattails, whistling out over the meadow and high
Above whitefaced cattle ranged grazing by fence on broken
    straw-bales
And still rising they slanted westward low over the wooded hill;
Now four dots in a line with a quiver of wingbeats veered
Quick left, quick right, circled once and paused, then darted down
Behind Bockius' Hill to land, we knew, on the long deep hole
Down below where Doe Creek flowed into Buck Creek. . . .

There were great wings nailed to the bookcase in the back of the
    schoolroom,
Over the glass doors of the bookcase, that opened and closed

On the shelves of lovely dusty books, where when lessons
    were done
And the upper grades at the front of the room on their long bench
Reciting, I could go back, and choose a book, and read.
I wondered about the wings, and a first-grade boy from over
Across Sand Creek in the hills said, "I think that's a
    heron's wings."
—He moved on wings wide and slow-beating over the meadow,
Rowing soft in the hush, in the rising sounds of twilight,
The noise of cows around the valley, voices calling them in,
Clanking of guineahens and bark of dogs in the fading light
On a stone by the water streaming silver through grassroots,
Falling in ripples through little pools where the pond-dam was
    broken
That my grandfather and uncles had made with a team of mules
    and a slip,
My uncles to help, the children watching and I—
How the slip went scraping and biting dry rocky ground,
The mules straining taut in silence, collars creaking.
Dust spurts from my grandfather's plopping feet as he pulls on
    the lines,
Strains at the slip-handles, chains on the doubletree jingling, slip
Digging deep as the team descends, biting into dark moist earth,
Slushing its fill in the lowest ooze, where the slip goes sleeking
A slate-smooth path with two creases, on to the turn and slow rise
Up the incline to dump the heavy mud. Later the slip
Lies rusting-red among stickerweeds, with their yellow flowers
Where bumblebees all burly in black-and-lemon fur
Becrumbed in pollen, would be wrestling of June mornings
To pack their thighs gold-tight with that sweet pollen
Before zig-zag-spiralling up, zooming heavy into blue skies
Between the garage and the chickenhouse where the mules were
    unhitched
That noon when the pond was made and we all came in to eat—
But now with the dam long broken, the pond in twilight,
I sat waiting for the bird to come down, very still under
A willow branch, with the rotten cool of the pond

Breathing on me, its July waters down to a pool
And black margin of muck between meadow and still water.
Three twilights I had come here to watch, had walked
Over the cracked mudflats, brittle under bare feet,
And stared at the bird's huge tracks by the water's edge:
And now the bird comes down, the great blue heron,
His long legs that had trailed like rope behind a rowboat
Reach forward and down stiffly, his long neck straightens
As the sailing wings cup and slow and he flaps drifting down
Almost straight down, beside the water; he lands, folds his wings,
Stands quiet watching; then stalks, breaking the pond's glimmer,
And stabs—at what! minnow or frog! I move,
And now his eyes look straight into mine, the wings
Go up and his thin legs bend, he leaps, whooshes upward,
He soars climbing the sky on his dusky wings. . . .

That time in May the birds would be just beginning at five,
The bob-white quail were whistling down towards the pond
When Mister Kendall drove up in the yellow truck to get me,
And I would be up and dressed and run out to meet him.
Driving the long mile back to the greyhound farm the light
Grew slowly, so by the time he'd parked and we'd gone down
To snap on leashes and bring the dogs out dancing up
On their toes, and up to the highway for their three-mile walk,
The east shone scarlet and gold, the air was brilliant, and up
The long hill to the valley's western rim with a pair
Of dogs on each hand, I'd not look back till we turned—
And when we did, and paused for the fast walk back down,
We had the valley spread out below in the morning;
I looked down on the highway, the lanes and the houses
    unshadowed
Till the sun's tip broke upward bell-vibrant
And thronged it with shadows, making the dewdrops glitter:
And that white house with its dark-green roof down in a meadow,
Set deep in its rectangle of prairie's translucent green, in the dawn
Glinting with dew, is my home, I know the very nests of its
    sparrows,

How warm, soft, scratchy-tickling their linings when I worm
  my hand
Wristdeep to finger thinshelled eggs or the naked pulsing bodies
Of young birds hot and tender and blind, to be dragged out and
  thrown
To leaping kittens that spit and growl baby growls through
  teeth that
Bring blood, spike-tails abristle, eyes glaring yellow and huge—
I know where the scissortails' feathered cup-nest is set in a
  solid fork
Of one catalpa tree on the front lawn; and that low limb
Where turtle doves nested four years ago with their silly platform
Of twigs from which one pointed egg fell, the other never hatched,
Though the plaintive whistling of their wings and ecstatic cries
  echoed
In the golden air of the west bedroom, twilight nearing, for
  two whole
Weeks of June: and where the concrete sidewalk ends at the path
  leading
Through high grass to the lane, where cousin Roy in the
  August dawn
Starting down to the highway for the morning paper, stepped off
  the walk,
Jerked back his foot and was missed by the darting copper head;
Roused us with screams and my grandfather strode with a
  baseball bat,
Swung, and missed it, and before he could pull back the bat
The snake had struck twice, leaving one fang fixed in the wood:
Dead, its slow writhing and belly-turning showed bronze,
  brown, gold,
Where the head had been was a smashed unmammal pink of
  raw stump. . . .
—My grandfather leaned in the kitchen door one day,
A short man with dignity and a quick violent temper,
Holding his heart, trying to breathe, while we all stopped
And waited. My mother's eyes were quiet, strained. Warm cake
  smells

Came from the oven; it was our birthday, my sister's and mine.
Grandpa had made the cake: my mother was sick in bed,
But rose to direct its baking. Of course it fell,
How could it not, with white Karo instead of sugar
And six children buckjumping through the kitchen!
Still, it was cake, sweet and heavy, satisfied our hunger.
He leaned there in the door with his mouth slightly open.
Suddenly he pulled himself straight and breathed;
Frowning, he never looked or spoke; once in the front room
Sat down in his chair and watched the fire, took out his pipe.
It was March-green logs, hickory and redoak sizzling, snapping,
Ooze of sweet sap brown on rough-sawn ends; the fire blazed hot
And popped little coals onto the hearth. He snatched up one
And puffed and drew the dry Granger's Twist alight with
    strangled hiss
—Dry acrid smoke, sharp unlingering smell from his soot-foul pipe.
We went next morning out to milk, Grandpa and I. Six-thirty,
Smoky lantern's light, through the chainfastened gate he had
    built, into
The lot. The Jersey cow heaved to her feet, breathing steam at the
    lantern.
"Head her off, Mikey." I trotted out and around her: "Go
    on, Bossy!"
She went, but snorting and bucking. "She's bulling already,"
    Grandpa said.
I was embarrassed. And Grandpa began to walk too fast; I had
    to trot.
At the barn, I let the Jersey in to her calf.
                        "Grampa, what are you
                        rushing for!"
He leaned on the swinging door, waiting for breath. "Well, I
    don't know,"
He said, "what's to become of us." After a minute we went into
    the stall.
I poured her feed; the Jersey came from her stall-corner,
    licked twice,

Tossed up her head. "Put the rope on this morning." I passed the
  slipknot
Over smooth curved horns, drew it tight. The whitefaced calf was
  sucking;
I shifted him teat by teat, in a warm smell of milk and calfslobbers,
Cowsmell and prairie hay's dusty herb-smell. In windy March
  darkness,
The barn was drafty, hay down to a few bales stacked around
  the stall,
The calf too young to eat it. Grandpa hung the lantern on its nail,
Leaned on the wall and watched me: "Put him out before he gets
  it all."
I grabbed an ear, yanked him ear-for-end, twisted his tail and ran
  him out;
He kicked up his heels and frisked round the lot in the
  greying light.
Grandpa was milking now, musky steam from the bucket's
  thick foam,
Shadows when the lantern swayed, holes the carpenter-bees
  had bored
In the two-by-fours of the wall. "Two gallons is all. Let him
  back in."
"Sook, calfie." He came plunging so fast through the door he
  bumped
The opposite wall, bounced off and trotted to her and sucked.
At once he flung up his head: "Look at him hunch her. Get him
  around
On her other side, and I'll strip her." I twisted his tail: around
  he went.
My grandfather stripped the last yellow cream into a saucepan.
He had to watch it: Jersey would kick when the calf hunched her—
Always on the man's side, not the calf's. He saved his
  half-pint twice,
And at last stood up. I slipped the rope from her horns,
Her I put out through the pasture gate, the calf into the lot.
The lantern's light had shrunk, I raised the hot globe and blew
  it out.

Grandpa carried the milk, I brought the cream, and the cats came
    running.
Behind the garage were saucers; milk poured from under its foam
    blanket,
We watched the kitten-bodies jostle, their modest pink tongues
    flickering,
And the eastern sky dovegray and crimson over the cold March
    pastures. . . .

Light comes faintly now: with a shock I can see the Cherwell
Or think I do, glimmering; and Magdalen tower is there, is
    surely there.
I sit on the wall's top, and from heavy wisteria vines a chirp,
Inches below me, sweet gurgle of thrush: it slips from its perch,
Flies busily up into a tall elm of the garden, and is gone.
Now here in the garden are singing blackbirds at dawn,
And a light goes on in the second floor of St. Alban's now.
That will be Gilbert Bray, my scout, washing up all the china
From last night's orgies: I'd best look in, maybe halt the damage
With a shilling for my part, before I sit down, sore-eyed
With memory flushed from this dark hour when I might have slept,
To puzzle out fifty lines of *Beowulf*—that dark poem
Whose hero plunged into the monstrous deep and down
Daylong to the dim hall under the waves where he found
The shark-witch's firelit lair, and felled and grappling drove
The brilliant sword through the bones of her neck till a great light
Flashed like heaven's candle and lit the hall, where he walked
And stared upon the treasures of long-forgotten kings;
While those watchful above, warriors who voyaged on foam-throated
Seabird over the waves to this wan shore, who would
Not leave their lord like the rest, look down fearful and proud
Where the furious waves grow dark with the blood of those
    monstrous things.

Sea-Changes

Birch Canoe

Red men embraced   my body's whiteness,
cutting into me   carved it free,
sewed it tight   with sinews taken
from lightfoot deer   who leaped this stream—
now in my ghost-skin   they glide over clouds
at home in the fish's   fallen heaven.

Stone Age

Whoever broke a rock first wasn't trying
to look inside it, surely,
just looking for an edge
or trying just to hammer with it, and it broke.
Then he saw it glitter,
how BRIGHT inside it was; noticed how things
unseen are fresh. Maybe he said
it's like the sky, that when the sun has
crashed down through the west
breaks open to the Milky Way and we see
farther than we are seen for once, as far
as light and time can reach and almost over
the edge of time, its spiral track like agate
swirls in rock from when it still
was water-stains, had not yet found its
non-solution to the puzzle
of dissolution, keeping within its darkness
the traces of its origin as day keeps night and
night keeps stars.
Pebbles, headstones, Altamira,
dust-wrinkles over darkness.
What shines within?

Geode

[A **geode** is a hollow mineral sphere sometimes found in limestone cave systems; inside, it may have crystals, often quartz, surrounded by layers of chalcedony. It takes millions of years to form a geode, which may begin as an oyster shell on a sea-bottom, whose cavity fills with a salt solution that is surrounded and isolated by a silica gel. The fossil shell is burst by the expanding geode; later, the silica gel dehydrates and crystallizes. Still later there is shrinkage and cracking, letting in water with dissolved minerals (by this time the sea-floor is part of a continent and it is ground-water trickling in), which crystallize inside the chalcedony wall. Rock shops often display and sell them, sometimes sliced into bookends or paperweights or ashtrays.]

I still remember ocean, how
she came in with all I wanted, how I opened
the hard shell I had made
of what she gave me and painted into
my lodge's white walls the shifting iris from
her wave-spray—
I remember even the vague drifting
before making a shell, my slow swimming
amidst her manna until I sank
down into stone, married, rooted there, joined
its stillness where the moving waters
would serve us what the moon might bring them with.
Growing, I remember how softness
of pale flesh secreted the smooth hardness
of shell, how the gritty pain
was healed with rainbow tears
of pearl,
I remember dreaming
of the new creatures flying through air
as the sharks swam through ocean,

hallucinating feathers and dinosaurs,
pterodactyls and archaeopteryxes,
huge turquoise dragonflies
hovering, shimmering, hawking after the great
mosquitoes fat with brontosaurus blood. And when
I died and the softness disappeared inside
my shell and the sea flowed in I saw
it drying as the waters ebbed, saw how my bony whiteness held
at its heart the salty gel whose desire swelled
and grew and globed against the limey mud,
chalcedony selving edged and spiked its way
through dreams of being flowers trembling
against the wind, snowflakes falling
into a desert spring. But the rain
of limestone hardened round us and my walls
grew full of holes, I waked into
a continent of caves, a karst-land where
sweet water chuckled and trickled, siliceated through
my crevices as once the salty ocean had, and I felt
purple quartz-crystals blossom where
my pale flesh had been.
Then I knew my dream
was true, and I waited for
the soft hand to come down like a dream
and lift me into sunlight, give me there to diamond
saws that sliced me in two, to diamond dust that polished
my two halves into agate bands.
I let them separate my selves and set them heavy
on either side of a word-hoard, whose light
leaves rustled with heavy thoughts between
the heavier, wiser, older lines of all
my residual selves, the wave-marks made
by snowflake-feathery amethyst ways of being,
by all those words,
by the Word,
made slowly into Stone.

Dragon-watching in St. Louis

for Stephen, Geoffrey, Vanessa, Lawrence

It would have been a dragon, this monstrous jet,
two hundred years ago, to father and little boy
come out for a stroll, had they seen it go screeching down
into the sunset with sweptback wings downglinting
as their words rose like drowned twigs from a stream,
the little boy exclaiming, the father agreeing.
They would have fled in terror what we take in stride
since we live near an airport and have rendezvoused
with sun and horizon here too often to fear
that this great beast might shatter, his smoky fires dim
the park, touched by the sun's last shining, we've come to see.

By the dark-mortared wall, whose chalk-white stones protect
this place from the fuming roaring freeway just beneath us,
we can look far over the asphalt and across suburban roofs
and see how the jetplane now small and tranquil is sinking,
winking the ruby of its landing light, in the last
seconds before it touches the earth beneath our horizon—
and we listen until it's come safely down like the sun,
till silence tells us it's landed, as darkness tells
that the trillion hydrogen bombs of our sun eyeballing space
to light and warm us this day have held their peace,
as firmness tells feet that the earth whose sensitive crust's
light quiver would bury us in our buildings, now smoothly
turns on appointed rounds as it brings this smoky city
gliding through sunset into starlit night as that dazzle of
cars weaving through traffic snarls, homing on supper smells,
tells us it's time to be strolling back home on the safe
sidewalks of this suburb
                              where bears and panthers, flood
and fire and that fearful monster the Wild Osage, whose blood
runs in our veins, ranged through these savage woodlands hundreds
of years ago, before the walks were made safe for us to enjoy
this zoo of smoky dragons now swarming from our best brains.

In the Changing Light

Brimming the trees with song
they flood July, spill over into
August pulsing lovecries,
cicadas here—one that
our cat brought me lay, legs folded
neatly, on clear wings as on a shroud, green
and white, fizzing now and then,
but when I threw it spread
wings and zagged in a wide curve into
the sweetgum tree where presently
that dry buzzsaw whined for some
significant other to auger down
into dark dense earth and gnaw at
the roots of things
sans eyes, sans wings, sans
song for seventeen years or so.

As daylight sharpens, deer slip back
into the woods, I wonder what a deer,
when danger grows too bright,
makes of a world whose darker,
truer memories in ear
and nose must solve the dazzle of
our alien eyes, more surgical
at stripping off its cover, at masking selves
as downwind leaves.
I've read somewhere the claim by computer people
that pain cannot be felt
until self-consciousness
has been achieved; and they had programmed in
that level, so they said, of artificial pain.
In A. R. Luria's book *The Mind
of a Mnemonist*, the man infallibly
remembered everything, but all perceptions

were unlike ours. Hearing, he tasted: sweet, bitter,
salty; heard neon colors; rough or silken, icy or
bloodwarm words: laid them like eggs aside on streets
his memory walked stolidly along,
walked back to get them when he needed to.
—Forgot, once, a word;
had set it carefully beneath a lamp
whose bulb was burnt out.
Bud opens and
is marigold, bird touched
by sunlight sings,
mind thinks:
I am. Still,
as the old man put it, coming out
into the light we wawl
and cry. I wonder,
in this darklit galaxy,
how that song is heard.

Foetal Research

I knew a man who peeked out from his genes
like a gorilla from its cage.
The funny thing, he said, inside there
was the one-way mirror where
he saw himself, and others saw him as
something he could not recognize
on which they did experiments,
and called it by his name.
They never came out from behind that darkness
but said he was exactly like the other
experimental subject in a cage they called
their neolithic time-dish. There, in vitro,
a chimp's egg had been fertilized
by Superman, and implanted in
an ethnic neighborhood.
It grew up Christian but was circumcised;
its molecules restrained,
he heard them say,
his twin.
Something inside him said
to name his children Jennifer,
Gerald William, Hezekiah, after his only aunt
and first wife's uncles.
The twin had children he called Jeanie,
William Gerald, Hazard Ira, after his two uncles
and first wife's aunt.
One fall they hypnotized the vitreous being and it came out
through the
one-way barrier to Milwaukee
where he lived. They had a glass of beer
and voted in the next primary, one
Republican and the other Democrat. In his heart, each knew the
other man
was right. Then the twin revealed

that in his cage there was a
oneway mirror too, and one time a cobra
slithered out and spoke to him. Any time,
it said, he would be welcome
on its side of the mirror. So would
his clones, but only while
they were asleep, because in dreams
they squeezed free of the cagy
crystals of time and words and spoke
directly to him.
But how (he said) could I
meet others who are not
ourself? That, the cobra said, is
easy. Find a two-way mirror, knock, and
walk on through. They'll call you Frankenstein, although
that's just a screen name, and you'll get
the Nobel Prize for them. Just say
I sent you.

The Man Lee Harvey Oswald Missed

In Berchtesgaden there was a doe with a fawn in the mountain
meadow behind our pension. They came out in twilight, the late
summer delicate light when mountain tops to the south and east
are still shining but the town below is alive with streetlights, and
the river noise comes up among traffic sounds and nearer voices
from the houses, hotels, villas that terrace down toward the town.
We had looked out from our balcony to white buildings on the
heights across the valley, Hitler's Eyrie. Then to our left, below us
and behind, in the corner of an eye something moved, the fawn
sprinted out from the woods into the meadow. Behind, cautiously,
came the doe, alert, trying to keep the fawn sensible. She turned
her ears like searchlights guiding her study of the scene, gradu-
ally stepped out into the meadow. They stood, grazed a few bites,
then the fawn darted on across, into the pines on the far side. The
doe trotted after, fading into the woods. We went downstairs, out
into the darkness, followed an asphalt path that turned to gravel
between dark silent houses, along the hillside, into woods. A mist
rose and covered the stars. We found a place to climb away from
the path, through brush and brambles, into a mossy leafy hollow
among tangles of roots and bare soil. Private enough, but not too
comfortable.

Next morning we drove down into town, then up the opposite side
of the valley to Hitler's old headquarters. The Bavarian businessman
and his wife had jollily directed us the night before when we came
back to a late dinner. Cigars and wine, broken English and German,
camaraderie. *Ja, das ist der Fuehrers. Amerikanische General hass
owned it now.* And it was true. **GENERAL WALKER'S SKYTOP**, the
huge sign before the turnoff said. The man Oswald tried to shoot
but missed, before he hit Kennedy. Who tried to stop desegrega-
tion of Little Rock or somewhere. Or was that some other general?
GENERAL WALKER'S SKYTOP, over a painted Stars and Stripes.
A tennis resort, skiers welcome; a museum. Muse-home. Clio, is
something burning? . . . . We paused in the parking lot and walked
over to the lookout place, stood by the low wall, looked down at
great busses lumbering like hippos up through the neat pines. We did

not go into the museum but drove out, past the huge American flag painted on its sign. What is the proper way to display the flag? Never let it touch the ground.

We had to catch a plane in Frankfurt. On the way we passed, near Munich, the sign that points to Dachau. In the airport, guards carried machine guns to protect us from terrorists. We bought chocolate and champagne to take home, and met no other terrorists. *Bin ich ein Berliner?*

A Response to Terrorists

It seems you can't
stay bottom dog too long
before some other bunch
outbottoms you. Frankly,
speaking as an Indian I admit
it's easier to be noble and smile
while vanishing, just as for Martin Luther King
in prison it was easier than
for Andrew Young as Ambassador—
and last war's victims of the Holocaust
are next war's seekers of Lebensraum
in Lebanon: the Palestinians are
the ones in concentration camps these days.
Isn't there some way we might
get out from under without finding ourselves
on top and smothering others?
Oh sure,
it seems unlikely that the Acoma
will buy out Kerr-McGee
and claim New Mexico as theirs, or that
the Iroquois will get the Adirondacks back
and run a leveraged buyout of
the Chase Manhattan, Rupert Murdoch, and the Ivy League.
But if they did,
would they be citizens at last of the great
imperial order, rather than our kind of
small endangered cultures where the sense
of needing every one of us,
of being the tip of growth, the quick
of living earth,
is borne in on us by our smallness,
our clear fragility?
It's feeling powerful and yet
afraid that fuels killing, it's knowing we are weak and brave

that lets us want to live
and let live.
The terrorists—
Reader, fill in the names of heads of government as you
read this: their names were once
(perhaps before your time) Reagan, Gorbachev, Shamir,
Khaddafy, Thatcher, D'Aubuisson, among the rest—
would they knife THEIR mothers,
shatter a GRANDchild's head against a wall or even
terrify kittens with a stun-grenade? They murder with
their tongues, send
surrogates to knife, garotte, beat, poison, torture—
who could count the ways? This is a tiger: fire off
a missile and the creature will
retreat respecting us. The kitten's
flayed, comes out a foot with self-inflicted
bullet hole, flapping like
a tongue. Forked tongue. Ah, look
how they leave the Summit, now,
climb in their stretch limos and drive away,
not skidding on the grandchild's brains.

How far from truth to beauty, say,
in diamonds?
Can we make either out of facts
put flatly, crunched together so their facets
crack light and spill
its rainbows over earth the way
plain carbon does when it is crushed into
a diamond, say?
A scientific fact was once
that stars made diamonds by their heavenly
"influence" acting deep within
the earth, mutating gunk
into bright gems;
but now it is a fact of science that earth
composes diamonds of itself—
and yet the earth itself was made
in superstars (another fact
of science, for the moment),
so that the house which stars once built
still crystallizes in the shape of stars, still
shines like them,
in language anyhow.
Of course
(you say) the earth, this common place, can't really shine.
But that's because we live too close to it:
the astronauts have seen
our muddy planet shine,
a blue star up in heaven.
That's what their eyes have seen:
their minds, of course, know very well it's not
a fact that's pure, it has
a flaw, depending on your point of view. It's air
that shines, and water mostly, earth

just holds these shining facts around
its heavy darkness.
So flights of angels, passing through our bodies,
may see a neutron shine
gemlike with facets, all the points of
inner structure netting
the radiant waves and fishing out
their rainbow messages of peace
from the God of Storms.
That, you'll say, is not
a fact—but if we just remove
the angels and insert
a physicist, you may allow
it is a fact though medaled
with metaphors and circumcised
by adjectives: . . .yes,
our physicist might say,
it is a fact
that neutrons have a structure,
and perhaps that each is like
a crystal, certainly
neutrons are being probed by beams of
some other particles,
and in the spectrum which comes back to us
from deep inside these specks of space
are messages concerning Universal
Creation and Apocalypse.
Thus far we state pure facts, although
they are imperfect when they're packed into
the seedy figures of our speech,
and blossom only in the arabesques
of math, which has no fruitful symbols for
Creation and Apocalypse except
a change of signs.
FACT meant SOMETHING MADE, in Roman mouths,
then English let it take the place of TRUTH.

Shakespeare was called, by Robert Greene,
"an absolute *FACTOTUM* in his own conceit."
He did it all,
that is, he *MADE* it all; instead of acting,
Shakespeare began to make the forms
for others' actions: yes, **FACTOTUM,**
that's the word.
People make diamonds now from coal, as easily
as they make perfume out
of oil, or pantyhose
from tar—
but diamonds we make
just as volcanoes did, with heat and pressure,
just as volcanoes were themselves
created by the moving
continents where the ocean's crust
dives under and the mountain-ship
floats over and begins to burn and thunder,
creating atmosphere, sunsets,
and diamonds in time.

And the male bowerbird creates his bower
to woo a mate, in fact the blue one chooses
only blue things to put in his,
he even mixes blue
paint and spreads it on his
bower's wall, using a piece of wood
or other brush to spread
the paint he's made from berries and
his way of seeing things.
But then, the fact is that
when once his mate is mated there
she leaves and builds her nest
and lays her eggs up in
some ordinary tree, and he just lets her go,
he takes no interest in the mortgage or the weather or the eggs, or in

those rising generations at their song,
he paints just what he sees, he makes
his gemlike house
of blue lights, keeps the species special and himself
fit to survive—and he's
a dinosaur, it seems, with warm blood, one
who put on feathers and survived—or so
facticians now assert as fact: the birds,
as Michael Castro says, are *DYNA-SOARS!*
If that is fact, we can no longer
believe that dinosaurs became extinct, just as we can
no longer hold that earth, not stars,
composes diamonds.
The trouble is, we keep exploding facts
into old myths, and then compressing myths
into new facts,
and so in this dark kaleidoscope
of headlined findings, what once was
crystal clear becomes too nebulous
to be believed,
—yet then becomes the evidence
that speaks of how our universe evolved,
as do the nebulae in space that once
were "clouds" and now are "ghosts"
of superstars that still broadcast the news
of brilliant bowers painted
upon the heavens long before
there was an earth
to sparkle bluely like a diamond in
the sky and make us wonder,
O twinkling little fact, just **WHAT**
you are: if true, how beautiful,
if beautiful, how true.

1. To The Eastern Shores Of Light

These neon lights are to stars
what Odysseus is to Dwight
Eisenhower—the way you've seen them there
at night, coming down to
LaGuardia over the glittering
inside-out cathedrals of
commerce under the dim
windows of your plane, looking down
past the massive tilting wing with its magically
shifting ailerons, its insect-like
adjustments, creaks and thumps that
keep us flying as we
drop downward cushioned against the screaming
hell of jets
just feet away, sinking into the fume
and grumble of traffic as we princes of
the middle air look at headlights like
souls gliding in Dante's *Paradiso* smoothly along
their destined ways, ruby
tail-lights among bright gold demoglyphs for soup
and motels, twinkling jewels that
Earth must be glad to wear, that make her
seem *fairer than the evening air*
clad in the beauty of a thousand stars—
and surely Marlowe's Helen
or Shakespeare's Cleopatra never
slipped into words more brilliant than
this *multitudinous space incarnadined* to which we now
descend with ordinary lives and dirty
socks, down into
glowing unreadable words which as we touch
earth gather into signs

of ordinary sleaze: close up, the city's like an
un-Midased Doppelganger of pond-scum that under
the microscope bustles with alien beings, just
dissolves and pretends
to be like us. . . . Bricks, asphalt, glassy hustle,
smog-dazzle, horn-blare.
But I was going to say,
when literature broke in with all
her fancy words about Cleo and Helen, not just that all these lights
are exquisite when seen
from far enough away, but that
so much of all this brilliance illuminates
our fear of violence and greed. I know that sounds
eccentric: what I'm driving at is how
these lights just aren't NEEDED
to spotlight things: no one would HAVE to see
the highways all that clearly, nor do showcase windows
along Broadway HAVE to be lit at night.
They do shine partly, I understand,
to MAKE us want
their jewels, airbrushed sex, their magic
carpets to the Hesperides glowing
in lightfilled windows—
but still,
each light-spell's meant in part to KEEP OUT
the smash and grab of those who can't afford
Hesperidean fruit, who'd settle
for just one crunch of the Big Apple, worms and all, wanting
the lineaments of gratified desire.
Looked down on from
a middle heaven, they are beautiful—but then,
those blue lights set along
the campus paths, they're RAPE lights, and
they are quite beautiful, aren't they? Messages
of want or violence down there, they all
look glorious from above.
NO, NO! JUST TAKE

those motel signs (you say): NOT placed
from fear, but Good Samaritans to heal the woes of
wayfaring strangers—and what's bought
by crown jewels spilling from Best Western
signs into our midnight windshields is only
hope, is comfort, bright enough
to see from far off shining there.
And that's true too.
And yes,
these signs of fear and
faith ARE costlier than Cleo's imperial gems and
snakes; the wealth of many continents must
be burned to set their many colors glowing, and they speak
the loveliest art our merchants of desire
have yet invented: one that transforms
a sleazy, murderous Times Square
of smogdom and Gomorrah into
Elysium by night, a brilliant mob
of souls *dwelling*
in possibility,
a fairer house than prose, and just
the place to go and become a star amid
the towered glitter that so many
blacklunged miners, cancerous breasts keep lifting
up toward the stars, high over
that sparkling babble of many tongues below.

2. New York, With Reservations

In the Hotel Empire's coffee shop
at Sixty-Third and Broadway
across from Lincoln Center, facing
the cold bronze back of Dante's statue
in its patch of pigeoned greenery,
we are waited on hand and foot, Stella and I,
then red lights part

the sea of traffic so we can cross
to a promontory flowing with honeyed singers
of Strauss, Stravinsky, Berlioz, where graceful
as a trained dolphin the Hudson River
leaps from the plaza's fountains, and on
a day of cold falling rain, a night
of icebound gutters, the seats
are plushy and warm, the stage
played on by lights that materialize
the Nightingale, danced by Makarova, and
the Fisherman, danced by Anthony Dowell, delivering
from death the Chinese Emperor—with singers
in dim orchestral limbo gilding with brilliant sound
the dancing lilies, until great storms
of applause conjure through parted
curtains the dancers, singers, orchestra
conductor . . . . and now the starburst
chandeliers relume, descend sparkling as
the audience rises, and we go,
Stella and I, into a special room
for Met supporters, and acting like
teenagers, have champagne.
—The people in this Belmont Room
are quieter, more silver-haired;
like Alistair Cooke they only grace
a Master Work, so this must be
Our Gracious Study. These waiters who are bringing
champagne, with one Coca-Cola for
the St. Louis friends who hailed us in the lobby,
are New York versions of
Lord Byron's best valet.
Elysium indeed: a hotel
not expensive, two days and
three nights of music, salmon mousse and hot
steamed chocolate with whipped cream,
a friend from Amherst who survived
the plane's crash off Cuba,

and nights in soft beds
with time and privacy and maids to repair, replace
each morning what is crumpled, soiled,
crumb-laden, wet, used up.
So when we exit, and come under
the green glare of Dante, we are not
yet ready to abandon hope, but flying as
gold-carded citizens within the Empire's
most affluent city we will depart
on shining wings and soaring above its storms return
to the Father of Waters and our small
teacherly tasks, driving Vergilian Rome and
Dantesque Florence into the heart
of this America.

3. On The Reservation

On a cold clear night in March, driving
through the Osage Reservation in Oklahoma towards
the old home, I saw
from the hill's crest down to the east
where once were miles of darkness under the stars
and moon, where wide
prairie and woods had held a firefly glow
of distant houses along the rutted
ungraveled roads, there now are blue-white
mercury lamps, whole constellations quilting
the soft darkness, at night turned on
by automatic switches,
blacked out by dawn. Beyond the prairie height
to eastward, where light had first spewed up around the new
radome and barracks of the Cold War's start, now
misting from the horizon is a smog of light
from Bartlesville that dims the stars.
I think it's the NEW WORLD rising
like midnight dawn, and it shines

only for safety, since weeknights by eleven
everything there is closed except
the lovers' lanes, and those (I hope) are dark. The hum
of generators laps our citizens
in light-cocoons. Maybe the darkness
between real stars is just too heavy, maybe
that makes us drag down heaven, hitch the fossil stars
of coal and oil and uranium
to our Volkswagens.
As for the cost, of course each burning light
keeps busy some poor soul, employs
the oil men, service stations, builders of dams and nuclear plants.
And if we try to dismount from
our star-striped tiger, we may slide
into his Heart of Darkness.
Ride him to glory, then!
And just consider
how all these things provide
new images for poetry, so needful if
the Epic of America shall be written; and
without an epic, EVERY empire crumbles. Even,
perhaps, WITH one.
And yet, wheeling
around the Osage Reservation with my one
surviving uncle of six, I was shaken
by what we saw, leaving Pawhuska: only
a vacant lot, dead neat grass around
the central square of earth where once
wine-red bricks of the old
hospital housed us when we were born.
Red local bricks or from
St. Louis that Grandpa Alex hauled
with mules, Old Beck and Jude, for the builders there.
Dissolved into thin air, an empty space where our folks
walked down the second-floor corridor to see the baby
brothers and sisters when they appeared, the little
Indian babies next to our mother pale and

darkhaired lying in
the hospital built when Pawhuska was just
a boomtown burning with oil and honkytonks and
swindlers, plenty of work for men
and mules, plenty of money flowing
through the Osage Headright families undigested to
fertilize the farms and bulging files
of lawyers, bankers, doctors, fattening raucous flocks
of workers hauling its bricks and timbers, all our white
uncles and Grandpa telding up hotels and
jails, and patronizing the latter
more than the former. And building
the hospital, where my Uncle Woody
once lay pillowed trying hard to talk, his tongue
split and his eyes black and swollen, his nose
broken from crashing that jalopy, but still happy
to see his sister Thelma's kids come visit him, then
as now. Yeah, I see
the night-light glowing in his room, his black
and purple bruises turn toward us, his sore mouth
crack to a grin as my mother
asked how in the hell it happened,
and his split-tongue lisp telling
how they'd come bucketing around the curve
at sixty miles an hour to see the headlights
on their side of the road and they had
to hit the ditch. And my mother laughing, glad
no one was killed.
Well,
it's a vacant lot, the new hospital's down
in Indian Camp, where the Pawhuska folks can go
and visit now the newly born, stove up or sick. Here
there's only a wintry lawn, the bed of scarlet cannas
gone that had always bloomed when
we visited. Things change, and so the pipelines
fan out grandly with natural gas and oil from here to
New York City. Beneath those mercury lamps, twinkling

out there in the Osage Hills, a family sleeps within
its pool of light, never on
the porch in summertime telling stories but
inside at the glowing tube that tells
of countries we are saving or creating over
one ocean or another, all
by courtesy of Babylon on the Hudson.

What was it like, I wonder, when
we bought this Reservation back from
the Cherokees, persuaded that the whites would never
covet these scrub-oak hills and rocky prairies, only
a hundred and twenty years ago?
The stories
were what we made, the stars we cast
ourselves into when we were named. Small wonder all
those city kids kept running
away to live with Indians, making up
new lives instead of being told them by some Bostonian or
New Yorker. How could they,
fleeing into our darkness, know it was death
they'd bring the elders in our lodges watching with
half-shut eyes how close the savage
empire was upon us, its sabred troopers ringing
our Reservation, barbarians on
the borders driving buggies over the line to picnic, choosing
the homesites for that day when earth
would be allotted, measured, sold.
So the outlaws flocked
among us, brought us News, Whiskey, Statehood And
Watermelons, made us the white
Forty-sixth Star blowing in
the wind. Join and/or die. So now
we CAN fly easily across
this continent where less and less
is dark and "empty." Maybe just to marinate in
the Dantesque brilliance of New York City's better

than frying in the friendly holocaust reserved
for our Lost Tribes. And so our
Empire draws us all together, all
our stories turn to HIStory, all the old
Republic's cities into one great city, waiting for that Vergil from
the distant provinces who'll lead
Columbia's heroes up to the Stars,
past Death itself they say.
But *you*,
they say, *pagan forerunners*,
you must go down again
into your Limbo: having (they say) served us in our need,
your proper role is now to
vanish: to be forever deaf
to all salvation's song, and without all hope to hear.
Someone, you know, must pay
for all the glittering
enlightenment we bring up from the dark below
this earth you had not used.

Snowflakes, Waterdrops, Time, Eternity and So On

for Bill and Carole, in Oakland, April, love and matrimony

They tell me every snowflake
differs from every other one,
               and yet,
so those who've looked insist,
they melt to waterdrops identical
each one with every other—
               this world I know's
a curious place, but who'd have thought those still
white mountaintops could capture difference,
those moving ocean waves identity,
while in between, the levity of clouds
keeps turning snow to rain or rain to snow,
and gravity's weird force has got us all
aspiring to disappear into
a singularity: who would believe
how those great powers wring
the music out of water over stones,
the rainbows out of waterfalls that silver
a mountainside with streams like veins
in a maple leaf keeping delighted eyes
from April sun—
green leaf trembling up here from loam
which over there has been called forth
as columbine and ponderosa: Listen, how all
those Trickster seeds and Coyote clouds, those
big bangers say
let there be light,
and darkness fountains dawn like
a trumpet's golden one-way where breath
goes in, Mozart comes out.
So let the two
be one,
snowflake and waterdrop,

tomorrow and today,
maple tree and columbine,
                              let us drink,
in fact, to weddings, bottoms up
with this sparkling champagne that is water
with a difference, its snowy bubbles briefly
dancing upon our tongues and rioting
within our veins and aching, it may be,
within our heads,
but not with grief,
not with regret, only
the knowledge that we'll have
our differences, and may
we thank God for them every day.

Sea-Changes

Phi Beta Kappa poem, University of Tulsa, 4 May 1990

For Don and Mary Frances Hayden

Where the electron gun targets the screen
between the past and us, we push
the buttons that will resurrect
The Living World within our living room, so that we
can watch dolphin and diver try
to comprehend each other's mind,
that ocean where each kind
doth straight its own resemblance find:
we sink down where
pale blue quivers as the dolphin swims
out of her dark shadows into
our hearts and minds. I think she hears mostly
a plume of silver bubbles rising from
this clumsy alien and the buzzing box he holds,
some glass-eyed thing that never, so far
as the dolphin knows, looks back—
yet here, from deep behind its glass
in our *dark forward and abysm of time,*
we sit looking into that dolphin's eyes and wonder
what goes on deep within her where
a consciousness of self and us might be. And words
come bubbling from our television, spoken
months later and thousands of miles away from where
diver and dolphin face each other, saying:
We tried to speak with dolphins. Knowing
they have a kind of language, we were hoping
to send a message.
—Now the diver has carried down into
the dreaming turquoise of
the dolphin's parlor ordinary jars:
they might be fruit-juice jars but in this medium they
transform, are sun-seines, crystal star-traps—and now

the diver takes his air-tube from his mouth,
inverts a jar and jams the tube up into
its mouth so silver bubbles fill
it with brilliant air and then
he does it to other jars, two, three of them;
and see, he's got a little rod to tap them with—
he's tapping, and we hear each jar
respond with different tone, he makes almost
a tune: it is enchanting—and look, from shadows there
offstage the dolphin eases toward his jars, she noses
past them, eying
the diver and the jars; she clearly
listens, and looks, and wonders maybe . . . ah no,
she turns, and her tail waves like a conductor damping down
to pianissimo, she swims away into the
darkness, saying with her whole body:
They'll never speak: they have no music.
Disappointed,
the diver descends now to the white fine sand
of the seabottom and glances towards the anchor-chain
of the boat he's dived from trailing there. He reaches
down, he picks it up, he looks: we see
the chainlinks glitter, hear the clinks
and scrapes, we see the anchor's flukes
unfold as he lifts it in his weightless dreamlit
heaven of Zuni silversmiths where he has set
turquoise atingle from that silver anchorchain—
and swiftly now from where
the blue turns black a shape comes hurtling, but
she turns and slows, she passes over the
jangling silver chain—
she looks, listens, she poises
quite upside down and drifts, beak slightly open, listens to
those tinny squeaks, clinks, scrapings, clanks: her eyes
lost in ecstatic hearing, her head as close
to the chain as she can get, saying
At last, a Tristan for my Isolde! how could they ever

encrypt this miracle of music in such links of light, who
could ever have composed it and was he the greatest lover of all
the dolphins in the world?

Well, OF COURSE!
We always knew the messages we sent
with Voyager would get across, though what
we didn't know was what the messages would mean:
the *Navajo Night Chant*, maybe that would heal
the wars out there—or would it take
the sound of crickets, or the clink
of chains in medieval dungeons? Perhaps the rasp
of dull razorblades across
a three-day stubble, or the screek
of chalk on blackboards,
THAT will be Beethoven,
our long-dead star rising to shine within
their Wave of Fame. *Humans,*
they'll maybe say,
they can't be ALL bad, if they can sing like that.

There is a down side, though—
could be, Beethoven's Ninth
and its great Ode to Joy
will translate as a declaration of
merciless war upon the beings of the first
palm-fringed star where Voyager
has washed up with our brittle jetsam.
—What did the Aztecs hear, when the white sails
of Cortez rose from a turquoise sea?
Five hundred years ago, we've heard,
Five hundred years ago Columbus came:
what messages our people then exchanged, what chains
of promises we heard. AND passenger pigeons, buffaloes,
Pequods and Mohicans heard: "we" sent "them"
tomatoes and syphilis, "they" gave "us"
the Civil Wars of aliens. So now we peer

into the eyes of natives trapped in the ruined walls
of Dresden, Hue, Beirut, El Salvador—

EL SALVADOR!—

paralyzed children staring
into the Pulitzer Prizes of our televising selves,
on Easter Sunday like flying fish
we skim the rainbow waves
of the Religious Channel purpled by the death
and resurrection of that Savior
whom Michaelangelo sculpted for his Pope—
breakfasting at home
we look down from within the dome
of St. Peter's there in Rome:
what music's there, what anchorchains
of hope, what alien sounds
we roll away the tombstones from, what alien eyes
we look into and try to comprehend.

When Earth Brings

For Joy and Daisy, grandmothers; for Simon, grandfather; for Rainy Dawn and Chris, parents; for Krista Rae, child; and for all our relatives

When earth brings the sun
into deep translucent
morning around us, when stars go quietly into
blue air behind him, we know
they are telling us:
Grandchildren, here is one of us,
we have arranged for you to see
the world you have been given on this day
by the clear brilliance of
our brother only, at this time,
but we are here, we have not gone away,
the earth will bring us back to you,
return us to each other and you will see
with our little sister's light, and all of ours,
how you move always among our many worlds,
the light and darkness we are given that
we give to you.
Dawn
is a good word to tell you
how children come into a world
again and again and how grandparents see ahead
in the blue dazzle where
a rainy light descends upon the earth,
where light comes back into the children's eyes with word
of how the earth meets heaven and how, one special time,
each child will look into the rain that lives
again on earth in a small pool and say:
I see myself, I see the stars,
now light and water give me back again
the world and heaven in which I live
and move and have my being,
here where the earth has brought
us everything, this day.

Carter Revard, part Osage on his father's side, was given his Osage name in 1952 in Pawhuska, the Agency town where he was born, by his grandmother, Mrs. Josephine Jump. He grew up in the Buck Creek Valley twenty miles east of Pawhuska, working in the hay and harvest fields, training greyhounds, and graduating as did his six brothers and sisters from Buck Creek School (one room, eight grades), where he and his twin sister did the janitoring in their eighth grade year. He graduated from Bartlesville College High, winning a radio quiz scholarship to the University of Tulsa, where he took a B.A. in 1952. He then took a B.A. from Oxford University with the help of a Rhodes Scholarship and support from Professor Franklin Eikenberry of the University of Tulsa, who also helped him go on to a Ph.D. from Yale University in 1959. Since 1961 he has taught at Washington University, St. Louis, and as Visiting Professor at the University of Tulsa and University of Oklahoma. His scholarly work has been in medieval English literature (manuscripts, patrons, social contexts), linguistics, and American Indian literature. Two collections of his poems have been published by Point Riders Press in Oklahoma: *Ponca War Dancers* (1980) and *Cowboys and Indians, Christmas Shopping* (1992). His poems and stories have appeared in many journals and such anthologies as *Talking Leaves* (Dell, 1991) and *New Worlds of Literature* (Norton, 1989).